D0866350

*Books by Anne Edwards:*

*THE HESITANT HEART*
*HAUNTED SUMMER*
*SHADOW OF A LION*
*MIKLOS ALEXANDROVITCH IS MISSING*
*THE SURVIVORS*

# The Hesitant Heart

# The Hesitant Heart

## Anne Edwards

Random House, New York

Copyright © 1974 by Anne Edwards

Library of Congress Cataloging in Publication Data

Edwards, Anne, 1927–
   The hesitant heart.

    1.  Dickinson, Emily, 1830–1886, in fiction,
drama, poetry, etc.   I.   Title.
PZ4.E247He   [PS3555.D87]      813'.5'4      73-5010
ISBN 0-394-48484-3

Manufactured in the United States of America
9 8 7 6 5 4

*For Catherine Edwards . . .*
*My loving muse . . .*

*Amherst*

---

*I felt a Funeral, in my Brain,*
*And Mourners to and fro*
*Kept treading—treading—*
*Til it seemed that Sense was breaking through—*

*And when they all were seated,*
*A Service, like a Drum—*
*Kept beating—beating—til I thought*
*My Mind was going numb—*

*And then I heard them lift a Box*
*And creak across my Soul*
*With those same Boots of Lead, again,*
*Then Space—began to toll,*

*As all the Heavens were a Bell,*
*And Being, but an Ear,*
*And I and Silence, some strange Race*
*Wrecked, solitary, here—*

*And then a Plank in Reason, broke,*
*And I dropped down, and down—*
*And hit a World, at every plunge,*
*And Finished knowing—then—*

# 1

*I*t was legend now. For over fifteen years Miss Emily Dickinson had not left her father's small estate. She was a recluse, a bit strange perhaps, half crazy, according to the village talk. When one did catch sight of her working in Squire Dickinson's garden, she was dressed in white robes and spoke to no one.

The judge had watched her grow from childhood to precocious adolescence, able to discuss politics and current events with her father's friends; bold in her opinions, original in her thinking, possessing such an intensity of feeling that not even the squire, with all his Puritan probity, could control it.

The judge felt his heart quicken as it always did in thought of Emily. He smiled to himself. He was not a handsome man, but when he smiled, which was often when not in his chambers, his craggy face lost half a century and he was once more a spirited boy. He had the same thick patches of unruly brow, the quick dark eyes, the undisciplined and full growth of hair. His bearing betrayed his more than sixty years. The fact was, he still felt young and vital. Even so, he and Emily had waited long enough. There were no obstacles now. Surely their unspent passion must not be denied.

Six months had passed since his wife's death, four years since the squire had departed, and nearly sixteen since he and Emily had been in Boston together. In all that time they had not been alone, nor exchanged a personal letter, yet in no way had that discouraged the judge's optimism. Only the Puritan inheritance with which the squire had charged his family could stand in their way.

Though years the judge's senior, the squire had been his good friend since his days at Amherst College. They had been a unique intellectual match, seldom agreeing, though always thoroughly enjoying the stimulation of their dissent. But Otis Lord had not been blinded to the role of tyrant that the squire played in his own home, nor to the way he treated Emily, making her his subject, his student, his dependent, his child, his—his, *his*.

Of course, the squire had been possessive of his other two children, Austin and Lavinia, but never to the same degree. Emily and her sister now lived with their invalid mother in the family house, while Austin had moved with his wife, Sue, and their three children to a small cottage on the squire's land, only an orchard away. Emily was in her mid-forties, but the judge still thought of her as a young woman. And the memories of the days he had walked with her beneath the apple trees and introduced her to Shakespeare remained his most vivid.

He drew back into the plush interior of the coach as its wheels shredded the alabaster stillness. It was the first snow of the year. The claret leaves of autumn had been swept away by November winds. He clutched the volume of Emily Brontë's poems he was bringing to Emily as a gift. She greatly admired the Brontë sister, and it was both curious and fascinating to speculate on whether she saw or imagined any likeness, as he did. There was the incestuous nature of the family circle, the homestead that was both haven and prison, the intellectual fervor with which they lived, Emily's secret writing, and the recluse life she had chosen.

Rumor had it that Emily had loved a man of the cloth whom she could not wed, and so had renounced the world. Judge Lord could not believe that was the case, for he recalled the electricity when her hand casually touched his, and the intensity, the depth of her eyes as she glanced across a room at him. Nothing could erase those many weeks they had spent in each other's company in Boston. Not even time. Emily simply could not have loved another with the same passion she had shown him. And the white robes and her withdrawal from society coincided with her return from Boston and followed his decision that they should not meet again. His own personal guilt, on this account, rested heavily. He had been a married man; a declaration from either of them would have been outrageous. He had followed the only possible course. Well, Elizabeth was dead now. He had come to free them both.

The coach was on the outskirts of Amherst. How unchanged it all was since his college days! No factory smoke rose above the trees, and the town was still composed of small farms clustered together. Even the population was about the same—a few recent Irish immigrants were all. And though it was one of the leading education centers in the state, students came and went but seldom remained or returned.

Life was filled with paradox. There was Emily confined to her fortress, yet with auburn hair full of sunshine, eyes like the finest, warmest sherry, a voice like distant running water, an unbound passion for nature, and thoughts when expressed that seemed always on the sunrise. She wrote poems like daily prayers, announced their birth and then kept them to herself except for small, teasing displays. There were her letters, of course, cryptic, difficult because they were really poems, and read oddly when paragraphed. He had to talk to Emily about that—about so many things!

Dear Emily, so bound by fear! He recalled the squire's funeral. Emily had not left the house to attend, but Austin and Lavinia had flanked the open coffin, and suddenly, Austin had leaned over his father's face and kissed his forehead and said, *"There, Father, I never dared do that while you were living."* And after the service the judge had joined the others at the house to extend condolences, and overheard Emily saying, *"His heart was pure and terrible and I think no other like it exists."*

No doubting it, the squire was as possessive and compelling in death as he had been in life.

The judge stuffed his present to Emily back into his pocket. Emily walked with shadows and she must be made to turn her step. There was sufficient cause for him to believe she was striving to do so. Which was exactly why he was on his way to Amherst now. Hadn't she written him a most encouraging letter?

*Dear Friend—I received your letter with great happiness —I have so missed your visits since Father's death. It has been four years! But of course, you know that! I have always looked upon your face as the very face of wisdom and have dearly missed our talks on books and nature which poor Father and my Boston cousins braved so courageously. I will be pleased to serve you tea at four on the day you will be in Amherst and trust my country manners do not prove too uncivilized for Salem's most distinguished Judge—Emily.*

The coach drew around a familiar cluster of trees. Sounds of living broke the stillness. People walked the streets. This was Amherst. Soon there would be an end to his speculation.

Emily took the front stairs two at a time. Her legs seemed too short and she was impatient to complete all her tasks. It had been a very special morning. The first snow! It was a sign, good, and heralding the future.

Father would have been very cross with her, and had Austin not gone to Springfield, he would be sitting in the parlor now. And perhaps Vinnie had some cause to be brooding at being sent to visit Sue. But conversing with Otis Lord with her father's spirit present was one thing, Vinnie and Austin quite another. What neither of them took into consideration was that death had seemed to condense their father's presence, and that the house remained as in his life—a house in which each member lived in his own world, yet each was bound to the other.

Downstairs, the rooms were filled with the warm scent of cinnamon and nuts from the sweet breads she had baked earlier. That pleased her, for the one remiss of winter was the loss of lilac and apple fragrance.

She hurried into the kitchen to set out the tea tray. From the window, the path approaching the house was visible. It was nearly four and shadow was turning the white to gray. Father's apple orchard stood beyond, stripped and shivering, but the kitchen was warm and cozy.

Emily sighed with delight. Usually her restraint was as rigid as Father might have wished. Self-denial was an honored virtue and self-indulgence a sin. But today she was having trouble tucking her heart "under." Her feeling of enjoyment at the thought of her expected visitor was so reckless that she feared it was most probably a sin—like gambling or apostasy.

The tray was done, the parlor clean, the fire blazing, and Vinnie safely on her way to visit Sue. Upstairs, Mother rested quietly. Everything was in readiness. She left the kitchen, thinking she might fetch her heliotrope shawl to wear about her shoulders. She was dressed in white, as she had been all these years. Would he, she wondered, remember that she had written him many years before that she would someday come to him in white?

The front door opened and a cold wind blew around her ankles. Slowly Emily turned. Vinnie stood in the front hall removing her cloak, her dark hair glistening with tiny flakes of snow. "Sue is not feeling well," she said, "I thought it best not to stay."

The two were small and of the same height. Vinnie was three years younger, but to see them together one would be convinced that Vinnie must be the elder. What a curious pair they were! There stood Emily in her flowing white robe, face to face with Vinnie, who was dressed, as she always was, in the style of her youth. The clock had halted for Vinnie when she was nineteen.

Emily stared at her sister with sharp accusation.

"Right, right," Vinnie managed, her voice shrill and nervous. "Sue is not indisposed, though it seemed to me she was a trifle disturbed, as she gets whenever she and Austin . . . well, when they have disagreed. But in all good conscience, Emily, I could not leave you and the judge alone."

"Otis Lord was Father's old and dear friend. He could never have anything but the proper intentions," Emily snapped.

"Intentions are one thing, Emily, a man's nature quite another."

"You have no reason to believe—"

"I have every reason! The judge was always drawn to you. I have eyes in my head! He came to see Father, but he remained to speak with you."

"Recall, Vinnie, that Judge Lord is now a widower and I am unmarried. And also, that Mother is in her room and this is Father's house."

"Perhaps you should recall that though Father is here with us, the neighbors might have difficulty *materializing* him!"

Emily laughed in spite of herself. Vinnie always had a way of turning a phrase so that it seemed humorous. When she was younger she had been a clever mimic. In fact, their shared sense of humor had enabled them to live in harmony for all these years, whereas much of her unhappiness over Austin was because he had misplaced his ability to laugh years before.

"I'll see to Mother," Vinnie said, and started up the stairs. She paused and looked back over her shoulder. "But I shall be close at hand." Then she tossed Emily a knowing look, held her skirts decorously, and marched up the steps and to her mother's door with a distinct military air.

Emily waited a moment and then hurried upstairs and to her own room. She took a sash from her bureau drawer. It was lilac-colored and made the dress she wore look like that of a young girl at a garden party. The grand old clock downstairs struck four. Emily picked a sprig of heliotrope from the plant in her window box and tucked it into her sash. The years had disappeared. It was Boston. No, it was earlier than that. She was sixteen and Otis had not yet married Elizabeth. He was coming to see her, not Father. She pressed close to the window— waiting, smiling, not truly needing her shawl, so warm was she with anticipation.

*         *         *

The judge walked up the familiar road with long, loping steps, stooping forward, his hands crossed behind, turning his head from side to side with a quick nervous movement. He entered a courtroom in the very same manner.

The snow was coming thicker, but he was rather pleased to have left the coach in town. The air felt good and bracing. Day had slipped away and there were lights in the houses: the Kelloggs, the Howards, the Cooks, and the Smiths. The judge smiled. No need for nameplates to tell you that folks here in Amherst seldom moved!

He paused. A light flickered in a window and a shadow moved and disappeared. "Judge Lord," the shadow would be saying. "Must be going to the squire's."

That was the way it was in Amherst. People lived their own lives, and they were very New Englandish, very Puritan in spirit—but that did not stop a man from wondering about his neighbors.

He could see the lights in Squire Dickinson's front parlor and he stooped forward again and quickened his step. He opened the white gate and walked beneath the squire's elms. Hurrying toward the porch, he slackened his step only when he was under the protecting eaves.

Then he stood up to his full height, wiped the snow from his face with a linen handkerchief, and clearing his throat as though he were about to present a verdict, lifted the heavy brass knocker and struck it against the great oak door.

Lavinia opened the door, but almost before the judge stepped inside, he heard Emily's slight, pattering step on the stair. Glancing over her sister's shoulder, he saw her.

Her chestnut hair in smooth bands, curiously nun-like in her white dress, she appeared to be gliding down the staircase. And the lilac sash, the matching shawl about her shoulders, the heliotrope she held in her hand added to that look of childlike innocence.

"These are my greeting," she said softly as she raised her hand to show him the flowers.

"We are so pleased to see you, dear Judge Lord," Vinnie interrupted. "You must know how saddened we were by Mrs. Lord's death. Mother would wish to extend those same sentiments and to welcome you as well, but her condition deters her."

"How is your mother's health?" the judge inquired.

"Poor," Vinnie sighed. "She is paralyzed and quite unable to do anything for herself. It's been that way since exactly one year after Father's death. But thank the Lord, her mind is as keen as ever and her hearing and sight as sharp as my own." She glanced over to Emily.

"Please convey my greetings." The judge removed his overcoat and Vinnie took it gingerly, holding its wetness from her.

Emily moved with nervous steps toward the parlor. "Vinnie does wish to be excused from tea if you will forgive her," she said carefully. "She has promised to read to Mother this evening."

"I am sure Mother would be agreeable if you cared for me to serve," Vinnie began hopefully.

"No need," Emily protested.

The three stood awkwardly, Vinnie finally turning away to hang the judge's overcoat in the front cloak closet. He took the opportunity to walk over to the parlor doors, near Emily.

"Well," Vinnie said when she was done with her task, "do have a pleasant tea."

"I trust I will see you before I leave, Lavinia?"

"I will insist upon it, dear Judge Lord."

Vinnie turned on her heel and slowly and stiffly mounted the stairs. Emily waited until she heard a door open and close. Then she entered the parlor. The judge followed her, and for a fleeting moment their eyes met. Emily gently pressed the heliotrope into his hand.

"Emily, it's good to see you," he said softly. He took the small volume of poems from his pocket and handed it to her. "I recalled your once saying how greatly you admired Miss Brontë."

Their fingers touched, and she pulled away as though shocked. She held the gift tightly grasped to her breast. "Forgive me. I hardly know what to say."

"That can't be right. There is so much we left unsaid."

She walked away and to the settee. "I was a foolish girl." She avoided looking at him and kept her eyes downcast.

"No, Emily, no," he said in a whisper.

She raised her glance slowly. "I could not look the world in the face, afterward. Bashful Pompeii!" She laughed nervously. "Perhaps it was wrong of me to confess my love. I knew Elizabeth was your wife, and I had no right—" Tears formed and she turned away. "I cannot fault you, sir, that you sent me home." She sat down, staring at the book in her hands. "I wrote you a letter immediately upon my return. But I could never bring myself to post it! *Dear Master—Have you the Heart in your breast—sir—is it set like mine—a little to the left—*"

"Exactly like yours, Emily." His deep voice shook.

"*If I had the Beard on my cheek—I wrote—like you, and you had Daisy's petals—and you cared so for me—what would become of you? Could you forget me in fight or flight—or the foreign land?*"

"I'm here, Emily. Doesn't that answer your question?"

"It poses more." She took a deep breath before facing him, her face and emotions checked for the moment, her voice cool. "I rewrote that letter so many times, I memorized it. Boston changed me. People now think me rather strange. I came home and this house became my Chillon. I dressed in white. I saw very few who came. Yet I wanted to see you more than all I wished for in the world. It's been fourteen years, Otis. Fourteen years."

"You haven't changed Emily. Nor have my feelings for you."

She could not suppress a smile. "I was so excited you were coming that I was sure I was committing a sin!"

"We have never committed a sin. Remember that."

She turned her glance to the book in her hand. "How fine you should bring me Miss Brontë!" she said, her voice not quite natural. "I have always said that when I die I hope someone reads one of her poems aloud: *Though Earth and Man were gone—and Suns and Universes cease to be—and thou were left alone—every existence would exist in thee.*" She held the book lovingly. "I hope I am not too depressing, speaking about my funeral like that." She hardly took a breath as she continued. "Mother is terrified of dying because she fears life everlasting. Though certainly, Mother has less to fear than most! I fear Father, but not life everlasting!" She laughed somewhat coyly. "I never have joined the church, you know?"

"That doesn't surprise me."

"It makes Vinnie very unhappy, but Father didn't press the issue. Well, you know that he believed wholly in the Bible and lived by it. But he claimed the church and the Bible were separate. The Bible had to be obeyed. The church was a private decision."

"I do remember that he never had another book except the Bible in the house."

"Did I ever tell you about the time just before Austin or I had gone off to boarding school and Austin came home with a book of Longfellow's that he had been given by a friend?" She only paused a moment, and when he did not answer, continued, "Well, he hid it secretly under the pianoforte cover, and we took turns reading it. I was in ecstasy. Ever since, if I read a book and it makes my whole body so cold no fire can warm me—I know it is poetry. And if I feel as if the top of my head were taken off—I know that is poetry. Emily Brontë's poems do that for me."

The judge sat down in a chair across from her and settled back. "What else have you neglected to tell me, Emily?"

"So much. There's Shakespeare. Or rather, the wise owl who introduced us." She leaned forward. "I could never forget, Otis, our walks when I was still a girl, and how you had memorized so much Shakespeare and recited it to me. I was sure you did so because Father would not allow you to present me with a volume. And Mrs. Browning—you gave me her as well. I knew what a great and splendid offering that was. I could not speak of such things before. But I have wanted to very much." She breathed deeply. "There is a great deal more. Will there be time to tell it?"

"I hope so."

Their glances met. "Emily," he whispered.

She looked down at the book she held. "I do wonder, don't you, if poems mind being so bound?" The room was hushed except for the crackle of the fire. "Father wasn't such an ogre. He did buy me books when I was grown, but then he begged me not to read them!" A smile flickered. "He feared they would joggle my mind, he said." She placed the small volume on the tea table, where he had set her heliotrope.

"Have you forgiven me, Emily?" he asked humbly.

"I cast no blame."

"Not even for the lonely years?"

"I am not such a recluse as the neighbors say. And I am far from unhappy. I have Father's house for the world, and for my companions"—her voice grew stronger—"for companions I have the hills and the sundown and the falling snow. And, of course, there is Mother and Vinnie and Austin and Sue and the children. And visitors come, as you have—and the post is most rewarding." She paused to study his face. "A letter is a joy of earth—it is denied the gods." Then, after a moment and in a shyer voice, she continued. "I have never been more joyful than when I received yours." She stood for a moment, straightened her skirts, and sat down again, primly, very much the hostess. "Shall I pour the tea?"

"Please."

He studied her as she leaned over the teapot. She

had a grace that he had almost forgotten. He was surprised that he had not remembered, for he could see her very clearly running through the fields before him, bending like a willow in the breeze, Carlo, the dog she had loved so, at her heels, both looking completely wed with nature. His thoughts went even further back to when she was a child and would climb upon his knee. *"Tell Daisy a story,"* she would say (that was her make-believe name for herself) and she would seem no weight as she rested her head upon his shoulder.

"I made the sweet bread myself," she was saying. "I always do the baking, and the gardening too." She offered him a slice of bread. "Vinnie was suspicious of your intentions," she said with childlike frankness.

Her chin was raised, her eyes unafraid. She had at last bridged the years and matters stood where they had during those long-ago days in Boston. It seemed the moment for Judge Lord to speak up, but he decided against it. He was certain of his own desires, but he had to be sure that Emily could cope with a proposal, would not shy away. So he held his silence and waited for her to continue.

"I must confess, when the time was approaching for you to arrive—I experienced a moment of fear."

"Were you frightened of seeing me, Emily?"

She rose and went over to the fireplace and stood in the warm and reassuring reflection of the flame. "Fears have often followed me in the dark," she replied.

"You are thinking about Boston again and that last meeting."

"It was a rejection. I never have been able to cope well with rejections. Just before Boston, I had sent some poems off to Mr. Higginson at the *Atlantic Monthly* to see if he felt they were worthy of publication. He rejected me, too. I have never been able to face a second rejection on their behalf. I write my poems and hide them in the back of my top bureau drawer. Not even Vinnie knows they are there. And I have hidden myself here in my father's house."

"Because of me?"

"Partially."

"I love you, Emily," he said simply.

"I will welcome you if you return," she answered.

He came and stood by her and their hands brushed and the judge could feel hers tremble.

"Remember how you read Shakespeare to me in Boston," she said. "You were my eyes and will never know what that meant to me. I went to Boston thinking I was going blind. My eyes were cured and my heart, too, learned to see."

"Emily—" he began, but she had stepped away.

The flames flickered as the parlor door opened. Vinnie entered. "Well," she exclaimed, "Emily cannot be so selfish! Certainly, dear Judge, it is only right to share your good company."

Vinnie paused midway into the room. She studied them both, a frown on her dark brow. After a moment, however, her eyes cooled and her mouth set in a smile as she sat and poured herself a cup of tea.

After Judge Lord's departure, Emily prepared supper and fed her mother. Then they ate in silence, finally bidding each other goodnight after Vinnie went to tend their mother. Once in her room, Emily paced the floor and stood before the window watching the falling snow. She lay wide-eyed in bed until the clock sounded two. The fire in her room died and she rose and wrapped her shawl about her shoulders. Lighting a candle, she set it on her desk. Her plan was to write the judge a letter, but for a moment she could not recall the date with which to head it.

*Tenderness has not a date—it comes and overwhelms—*

She put that piece of paper aside and took another.

*My lovely Salem smiles at me I seek his face so often—But I have done with guises—I confess that I love him—I thank the maker of Heaven and Earth—that gave me him to love—the Exultation floods me. Oh nation of the soul thou hast thy freedom now—*

Her hands were chilled and she found she could not continue. It was not in her best handwriting anyway. Taking both slips of paper, she replaced them in the desk drawer. She would write the letter when the sun rose.

*3*

$O$tis Lord's name had long
been a synonym for strength and power, not only in his
own Essex County, but in the entire state of Massachusetts. He was known for upholding the minority view-
point. He had fought tenaciously for the election of Webster for President and severely challenged the formation
of the Republican Party. His unsparing cross-examina-
tion had ranked him among the foremost men of law in
New England. In most houses in the state his was a
familiar name, and there were few homes that he could
not have entered and been able to strike up a warm and
immediate friendship. Yet, it was curious how much a
stranger he felt on his own threshold.

The house stood on the corner of Lynde and North
Street, a short distance from the Salem Witch House. It
was not one of the superb old houses that gave the city
its charm, for it had been built to his wife's unimagina-
tive specifications. It was substantial, comfortable, and
designed with household efficiency in mind. Little more
could be said.

He stood waiting in the hallway as though he were

a guest, as if it would be an intrusion to go deeper into the house without being escorted. After a moment he realized no one had heard him enter, and hurried to his library at the rear. The room had a bay window that in summer looked onto a rose garden. Originally it had been the dining room, but it was the brightest area in the house, and after Elizabeth's death the judge had turned it into his study.

Although the house was not harmonious with his creative nature, until the time of his wife's death it had at least been quiet and relatively peaceful. They had been childless and Elizabeth never enjoyed the role of hostess. It was all quite different now. Following Elizabeth's funeral, her widowed sister, Mary, and Mary's daughter, Abbie, had come to care for him. Now the place prattled with their goings and comings.

In his opinion Elizabeth should have married his older more elegant brother, Nathaniel, who possessed the polish he lacked. The judge knew he was a strong man, strong in his emotions, his friendships, his loyalties, his prejudices, and strong in thought and in language! His deeply passionate nature had offended Elizabeth, and she avoided as many confrontations as were possible.

He sensed these same passions in Emily. Unlike the friends and neighbors who received her verse or prose without understanding, he was certain that she was touched with genius. He was, in fact, overwhelmed by the beauty of her language and the power and incisiveness of her thought.

It was weeks since his trip to Amherst, but they had begun a loving ritual of exchanging letters. On the day hers was due he would set aside sufficient time for a reply. But today, when he should have received a letter, there had been none.

Of course, it was presumptuous of him to feel that Emily in any way had been remiss, or that her time should be committed to his desires. He knew very well how hard her life was, how filled with daily tasks and responsibilities. It was a miracle that she found time for her poetry. Even though she protested that she now did the butterfly and not the moth tasks in the house, the judge was aware that her life was a great deal harder than a woman's life would be in a city like Salem. Amherst was still somewhat primitive, still farm country. Although the Dickinson women no longer had a man to tend, they also did not have one to bear the weight of heavy duties. The judge resented the harsh life Emily led, but admired her the more for bearing with it.

There was a knock on the library door. "Come in," he called out.

His niece, Abbie Farley, stood in the doorway.

"Well, come all the way in," he commanded.

Abbie at twenty-six had already taken on the mantle of spinsterhood. Though she was never pretty, the judge could recall the few fresh years when her dark hair and even darker eyes had held promise. Now, not even a ghost of it remained. She was small, which gave her an air of feminine delicacy, but she moved stiffly and with a starched *swish*. Her presence in the house would have been completely intolerable were it not that she was more efficient in the running of it than Elizabeth had been, and certainly a damned sight more organized than her mother! Also, and as a compensation for her other abrasive qualities, she had a most unusual and pleasing voice, low, and though clipped, quite musical.

"I trust, dear Uncle, you will accept what I am about to say in the spirit it is meant," she began.

The judge sat forward in his chair, as he often did in court. She had paused. "Go on," he told her.

"As I had early errands to tend, I thought it might be of service to collect the post as well. I went directly there so that I could do the shopping on the return."

"Quite sensible," the judge agreed.

"There was a letter from Amherst, but before Mr. Cully gave it to me, he held it deliberately in his hand for a moment and studied the writing on the envelope. 'Come regularly, don't they?' he said, and I might add, in a very insinuating manner."

"That was the entirety of your exchange?"

"I most naturally did not reply, but took the letter and left without a backward glance. Insolent!"

"May I have it?"

She took it from the pocket of her heavy skirt. Her starched linen cuff grated the coarse dark fabric. Her wide hands and broad nails offended the judge. The small blue envelope changed hands. "Thank you, Abbie."

She did not move. "Out of duty and love, dear Uncle, there is something I must say."

"You did not swear an oath." He smiled wryly.

"But I did! When out of your goodness you took my mother and myself under your roof."

"A man is indeed lucky when he has womenfolk to look after his needs with the efficiency that you and your mother have administered."

She stepped closer to him. Her hands gripped one another resolutely. "Miss Emily has always been kind to me when I have visited Amherst and called upon her," she said. "I therefore do not mean to be unkind by what I am about to say, nor disrespectful, since Miss Lavinia is a dear friend of my mother's. But—Miss Emily is indiscreet. That is her nature, and a serious defect. She must know of the potential gossip—idle or unfounded though it may be—that can arise from a man of your fame and stature receiving regular letters with her name so boldly written upon them as sender."

"You have spoken, Abbie. Now you can leave to complete whatever task this has interrupted," the judge answered angrily.

Abbie remained implacable. "She is strange. And they speak about it not only in Amherst but in Boston and Springfield—and Salem, wherever she sends people those curious poems." She raised her chin with a touch of smugness. "Miss Lavinia told me that she lost her true love when she was a young girl and that had unsettled her. Even so, dear Uncle, a man of your reputation and generous nature should not be subjected to her indiscretions."

"Abbie—" the judge warned, his glance harsh and his voice sharp.

Abbie dropped her hands to her sides but stood her ground. "The needle not the pen is the instrument for a woman," she said. Then, nodding her head, "I apologize, dear Uncle, but I know you admire honesty and would not have less in your home."

Turning, she left the room, making sure to close the door behind her, and hastened to the sewing room, where her mother and Mrs. Bowser, the seamstress, were sewing. "May I speak with you, Mother?" she asked anxiously.

Mary Farley was immediately alerted. She put down her work, and begging Mrs. Bowser to excuse her, followed Abbie out into the hallway. There was little resemblance between mother and daughter. As plain and ponderous as Abbie was, her mother was fair and slim, taller, delicately put together, and much to her daughter's distress, given to the vapors on the slightest provocation.

"What is it, Abbie?" her mother asked, her hand

already poised half expectantly on her breast.

"Uncle received another letter from Amherst this morning and I spoke with him about the gossip."

"Oh *dear*, you should not have done that. No. It was quite indecorous." She reached for her lace handkerchief, and though the hall was unheated and chill, began to wipe her brow with it.

Mary Farley could not bring herself to reveal to her daughter her true concern, one that had to do with the indelicate subject of money. Mary and her daughter were quite without funds, but as she proudly insisted, not without prospects. It was an acknowledged fact that the judge's outright manner had caused severance with his own kin, that she and Abbie were amply provided for in his will, and that since his own nieces were wealthy in their own right, and he had no children, Abbie would be his heir.

"You should not upset your uncle. You must remember he has a great many very important matters on his mind. We should always work to create a harmonious and pleasant home for him."

Abbie did not seem to be listening. "He can't go to Amherst alone again. If he marries Miss Emily, I shall never forgive myself."

"Marry . . . Emily Dickinson . . ." Mary Farley swayed forward.

"Don't worry, Mother," Abbie consoled as she supported her. "We will, of course, go—if there is a next time. Meanwhile, perhaps it would be wise to keep in closer contact with Miss Lavinia."

"Dear me. Yes . . ."

Abbie took her mother gently by the arm and helped her back to the sewing room. It would not do for Mrs. Bowser to sense that anything was amiss.

\*     \*     \*

The judge held the envelope for several minutes before opening it. Then he studied the careful, graceful script. Emily must have copied the pages several times before they had reached such perfection.

He read softly, aloud:

*"My Darling Salem—Tuesday is not far enough from your dear notes which arrive each Monday—for the embryo of another to form—and yet, what flights of Distance—and so I perish softly and spurn the Birds and spurn the Sun and with pathetic malice—but when the Sun begins to turn the corner Thursday night everything refreshes—the soft uplifting grows till by the time it is Sunday night, all my cheek is afever with nearness TO YOUR BLISSFUL WORDS. It is strange that I miss you at night so much when I was never with you—but punctual love invokes you soon as my eyes are shut—and I wake warm with the want sleep had almost filled. The clock in the hallway has just struck one and all is still as the stern profile of a tree against a winter sky. It is cold and not even the wind dare breathe. I hope you wear your furs tomorrow. Those and the love of me, will keep you sweetly warm though the Day be bitter. The love I feel for you, I mean your own for me—a treasure I still keep—Your Emily."*

The judge returned the letter to its envelope. Then he unlocked his desk drawer and placed it lovingly on top of the others Emily had written him.

He had reached a decision. He would write to Austin Dickinson and petition for Emily's hand, and he would return to Amherst.

*4*

*E*mily was grateful that the well was under the house and not outdoors, as it was in most houses in Amherst. Still, the kitchen pump was old and difficult to work, and her arms were stiff. The day was bitter cold and she had been up since dawn feeding the fires, baking the bread, tending her mother, cleaning the whale oil lamps, and finally, preparing the midday meal. Her heart could not be repressed though, for in just a few days it would be Christmas, a holiday she dearly loved.

Her heritage kept her from preparing for it as she secretly wished. In her grandfather's day, and in the Puritan world, to celebrate Christmas had been a penal offense, and certainly her father in his lifetime considered it so. As she sadly remembered, he had frowned upon Santa Claus and all such prowling gentlemen. Of course, Father had been a Congregationalist, and Christmas, with other holy days, was rejected by Congregationalists on the ground that they adjoined on no higher authority than that of men. They did not even see cause to believe that the day was the true anniversary of the birthday of Our Savior!

Emily wished that Austin's children might at least

hang up their stockings. She had spoken to Austin's wife about it, but Sue would not consider so openly defying him (though in small ways she did so as often as was possible), for she knew he believed Christmas Day a joint device of the Devil and the Romish Church for the overthrow of the true religion and, therefore, to be frowned upon by all good people.

But no one could halt the celebration nature hosted, nor the great joy Emily received attending it. From the kitchen window she could see the smart line of evergreens that blocked the view of Austin's house. The trees were laden with snow and stood white and proud, the morning light making them glisten and sparkle as no false ornaments could do. On the previous night, from her bedroom window, the church steeple had looked like a silver sleigh slipping its polished tip into the field of stars.

She put the kettle up and fed the stove more wood. She hardly felt the weight of her heavy skirts as she hustled about the kitchen. The holiday was only a short few days off and she could not stifle the anticipation with which she had been marking the hours until its arrival. She felt the same emotions as when, twenty-five years before, the circus had come to town, heralding its arrival with the announcement:

OUR ENTRE INTO AMHERST WILL BE
OF A GRANDEUR BEGGARING DESCRIPTION!
A TRIUMPHAL ROMAN PROCESSION! THE
KOSSUTH CAVALCADE WITH PRINCIPAL
LADIES AND GENTLEMEN IN FULL
HUNGARIAN COSTUME!

She had watched the circus parade from the house, and though the drums were long silent, could still feel their beat in her mind.

Sue, who had been upstairs visiting her mother-in-law, joined her now. She sat at the kitchen table, the winter sun giving the illusion of crystal threads in her graying hair. They had been sixteen when they met, and both were still surprised to be confronted with the reality that so many, many years had since passed.

Time had not dimmed Sue's prettiness—even now as she frowned. "I was just thinking back to when we were very young and how gay and romantic Austin was then. That Austin seems so far away now."

"Funny"—Emily nodded sadly—"I often think about those days, too, and wonder if some trick of time has suspended both you and me, leaving us forever in our summer dresses, while Austin . . . Austin somehow was dragged helplessly away to a distant winter that seems to have left him leafless." Then, hearing her own words, she sprang to her brother's defense. "Of course, he has so much responsibility. Carrying on for Father at the College, managing financial matters for all of us, and sheltering us." She stirred the corn chowder as she continued. "He has, as Father would have wished, given all us Dickinson women time for our own thoughts, saving us from the worldly humdrums that would have rendered us leafless, too!"

"It's no good cloaking Austin with so much righteousness, Em," Sue scolded. "Nor concealing the obvious." A look of pain crossed her face. "Austin is a very . . . *cold* man, Em, and I am freezing for want of the sun."

"Oh, Sue . . ." Emily turned and her eyes brimmed with tears. "Surely the children bring much happiness," she whispered.

"Oh, yes . . . the children." Sue sighed.

Both women turned away, embarrassed and made silent by this unusual display of emotion.

"I baked a plum cake for them," Emily said at last in an attempt to lighten the mood.

"I think sometimes, Em, that you are but a few years distant from them and very much part of their generation," Sue teased.

Emily was laughing. "I often feel that way myself!" She covered the chowder and added some molasses to the beans and then sat at the table with Sue. Her hands were clasped together and resting on the thick oak edge. The laughter was gone but its reflection lingered in the depths of her eyes.

"Perhaps none of us are as we were except in memory," she said, her gaze finally settling on Sue's well-loved face. "I am no longer sure I am to Austin that same Emily who wrote him confiding and feverish letters when he was away at school, and who shared escape and conspiracy from Father's diligent care. If I could have remained that same Emily, I would certainly have done so. And Austin—*yes*, I believe he would have selected to remain that same Austin." She rose to her feet, but as she did so, her step faltered.

Sue was instantly at her side. "Are you ill, Em?"

"No. It is just that so much has occurred—so much —these long years, I staggered as I thought of it." She sighed wistfully and moved away and to the window.

It was a moment before Sue was able to reply. "I try to remember that, and most times I succeed," she said softly. "If I did not, well, I don't know—but remembering how Austin and I once walked hand in hand helps me to endure. Yes, it does that. But again, it also makes the absence of his touch now almost unbearable." She turned away and busied herself about the kitchen. "Vinnie tells me you have been corresponding with Otis Lord quite regularly."

"Yes."

Emily was back at the stove and the steam rose about her as she lifted the covers of the huge pots and stirred their boiling contents. She did not reply.

"Vinnie is worried lest you should forget decorum," Sue added.

"How could that be possible when she is so constantly reminding me we are two old maids?"

"Em, you are not!"

"Of course I am. And so is Vinnie. But who knows about tomorrow?"

"Em, are you *entertaining, considering?* No! Has the judge been *intimating?*"

"There's Vinnie coming up the path," Emily answered, relieved to be able to distract Sue. "She looks half frozen! Make some of your best coffee, dear. I'll go greet her."

Vinnie was blue with cold and her skirt hems were heavy with snow.

"You will catch your death," Emily warned as she took the parcels from her sister's numb hands. "The stove is hot. I'll heat some water. In the meantime do take off those wet clothes. There is a lovely fire waiting in your room and Sue is just putting up a pot of coffee."

Vinnie nodded her head and started up the stairs.

"Oh, Vinnie—was there any post?" Emily asked.

Vinnie did not pause until she was at the top of the stairs. "Yes," she called down, not waiting for a comment from Emily as she turned swiftly on her heel and disappeared into the darkness of the upstairs corridor.

The kitchen was thick with the smell of coffee and molasses. It comforted Emily as she rejoined Sue. "I must go," Sue said. The two women linked arms and went out into the hall. "Em—" Sue began uneasily, "don't let them dissuade you."

"Who dear?"

"Vinnie, Austin. About Otis Lord, I mean. They like you home to return to—as your father did. They resent change or any new circumstance."

"I'll remember."

"And, Em, I understand where others might not, that with your books and your poetry, the letters you write, the visitors you choose to see—you are less of a recluse than the other women in this town who are locked into the severity of their lives. And also, that it would be a waste of time to talk with them. But *Salem* and *Springfield* and *Otis Lord's circle*—Em, that is another world, and you would do well to discover it."

Emily smiled and the two women hugged each other. "Oh, Em, I am just so weary of all the elderly people Austin is friendly with at the College! Everyone all dressed in dark colors, having their suppers always at six o'clock, not playing cards, nor dancing, nor discussing any writer or philosopher who has not been dead a hundred years! And they think you 'queer'! The world is upside down with madness!"

"Emily . . ." Vinnie called from upstairs.

"I'll be right there, Vinnie," she answered. "Oh, Sue! I quite forgot!" She ran back into the kitchen and reappeared with a beribboned parcel decorated with candy stars. "It's the plum cake for the children," she told Sue. "And if I could, I would have plucked a real star for the top. Tell them so for me," she whispered.

"Has Sue left?" Vinnie asked when Emily brought a kettle of hot water to her room a few minutes later.

"Yes," Emily said as she filled the basin at the side of Vinnie's bed.

"It was certainly foolhardy for me to go into town today, but you seemed so insistent," Vinnie complained, and submerged her bare feet in the water as she sat on the edge of the bed. "Though Glory knows, if I had not filled your list the world would not have come to an end."

"I'm planning some special baking tomorrow. The shopping couldn't wait."

"You were also expecting a letter and *that* couldn't wait!"

"Oh, Vinnie . . . where is it?"

"On my bureau."

Emily fetched it hurriedly and then, without a glance at the envelope, slipped it into her pocket.

"The least you could do after I exposed myself to pneumonia and Heaven can only guess what else is to share the news," Vinnie said petulantly.

Emily took out the letter, and breaking the seal carefully, opened the envelope. "It's from Judge Lord," she said quietly. And then, after a longer time than it would take to normally read so short a note, "The judge and the Farley ladies will be in Amherst day after tomorrow."

Vinnie sighed with relief. "How very wise that he isn't coming alone."

"Was that of your doing, Vinnie?" Emily asked as she refolded the letter.

"Mary Farley did write me a few days ago and mentioned how long it had been since she had seen us all. I am so fond of Mary, as we all are, of course. Most naturally, I replied asking her to visit whenever the judge should come to Amherst."

"You had no right, Vinnie," Emily replied sharply.

"Someone must remember propriety," Vinnie countered.

"I should have been consulted."

"Sorry, dear," Vinnie trilled.

"I will not see Otis with chaperones present, Vinnie, so I suggest you speak to Austin and Sue and see if they will have the Farley ladies to lunch on the day after tomorrow." Emily started out of the room. "I am going to fetch a kettle for Mother. Perhaps when I return you would help me to bathe her?"

"Of course, dear," Vinnie said sweetly.

Vinnie listened to Emily's slow and hesitant step as she descended to the kitchen. A small pain clutched at her chest. She loved her sister very much and it was almost more than she could bear to see Emily unhappy. But whatever she had done was in Emily's best interest. Loose talk simply was not.

Emily had read the words in the Bible so often that she had only to glance at the text from time to time. She sat stiffly by the side of her mother's bed, still disturbed over the confrontation earlier in the week with Vinnie, and unable to forget that this was the day that Otis was due in Amherst.

Her eyes were not on her mother's pale, emaciated face, but on the bedside table where rested a daguerreotype of her father made in 1853, when he was not much older than she was now. She was overcome for the moment with the feeling that it was more a presence in the room than the withering creature pillowed in yellowing hair to whom she was reading.

The photograph showed the firm set to her father's mouth, his piercing, winterbound eyes, his high-domed forehead and his thick bramble of hair that grew wildly and seemed harassed by gale winds. Her father would never have approved of Otis Lord as a suitor. She knew this with all her heart, and as she studied his image—the head held so stiffly and braced in a formal black suit— she was surprised at the fear her father could still raise in her.

There were tears in her mother's eyes. "Oh, Mother, I'll stop reading if it disturbs you," she said.

Mrs. Dickinson spoke in a whisper and the words came very slowly. "One must not close one's ears to the sound of pain—even Job's," she said haltingly.

Emily patted the wasted hand and then held it in her

own. *"For now should I have lain still and been quiet,"* her voice continued in automatic recitation. *"I should have slept: then had I been at rest. With kings and counsellors of the earth, which built desolate places for themselves; or with princes that had gold, who filled their houses with silver. Or as an hidden untimely birth I had not been; as infants which never saw light. There the wicked cease from troubling; and there the weary be at rest."*

Her mother's eyes were closed, her breathing shallow. She seemed to be asleep. Emily slowly withdrew her hand and closed the Bible and rose as quietly as she could, but the old lady fluttered her lids and whispered something. Emily had to lean in very close to hear what she said.

"What is it, Mother?"

"Secrets . . ." her mother sighed.

Emily smiled down at her. "You should sleep now," she said.

"Sleep frightens me."

The old woman breathed deeply and with tremendous effort. Emily drew closer and waited.

"Your father," the weak voice began, "was intelligent. I knew . . . I knew . . . I understood. I had so much *less* to give, and you . . . you needed, *still* need, so *much.*" She breathed unevenly for a few moments before continuing. "Still, this much I know. Love is more than . . . knowledge . . . and a woman withers without it." She closed her eyes and Emily thought she might be done speaking, but further strength came from somewhere. "Secrets, beyond my door, in your father's house. They exist in your heart, in Lavinia's, where I . . . I cannot seem to reach them. Never could."

It seemed she wanted to go on speaking, and indeed, must have been conversing silently in her mind, for from time to time she would nod her head or sigh, and after several minutes a tear rolled down her wrinkled cheek.

Emily wiped it gently away. "I will be back shortly," she said softly. "You rest."

She had never been able to come to terms with her feelings toward her mother. Though they looked alike and bore the same name, they were strangers in all else. Moments before she had blamed herself; now, the house so still, alone except for the sleeping old woman, she began to sense the truth. Her father had kept them strangers. His country had been the mind, and he had ruled absolute. There had been no place for divided loyalties.

She returned to her room, pacing it, allowing the fire to fade to embers. Salem was but a hedge away, and here she was imprisoned by her own, her hesitant heart. Somehow, her mother had known. There was no explanation for it. She had never discussed Otis with her mother and doubted that Vinnie had—but her mother *had known.*

There was insistent knocking on the front door, and Emily, thinking only that her mother must not be disturbed, rushed down the stairs to open it.

"I am quite alone," the judge said as he faced Emily's startled glance. "May I come in?"

## 5

ears earlier Emily had learned to keep her emotions under control. She had succeeded so well that neither Austin, Sue, nor Vinnie was aware of the intensity of her emotional life. Her father had trained his children to understand that they were bound in all but thought. He had shared everything but his soul, and if anyone tried to probe his "inner being" or was indelicate enough to approach the "intimate," he withdrew.

It was the pattern of behavior Emily was accustomed to, one she felt safest adopting, and one from whose path she seldom veered. However, as she stood facing Otis Lord in the stark no-nonsense entranceway, she could not believe her own lack of composure.

Emily was well aware that she had grown to the plainness her early years had promised, that though her hair was richly colored and her skin almost transparently white, her mouth was still too wide and her upper lip too long for beauty. She faced Otis Lord, unsteady on her feet and unsure of herself.

She turned aside to conceal her discomfort. "I

haven't built a fire in the parlor. I wasn't truly sure you would come." She thrust her hands into the pockets of her white robe to hide their trembling. "But we can go into the kitchen." She spun on her heel and led the way. "Mother is sleeping. We wouldn't want to disturb her," she added.

The room glowed with warmth and the teakettle sat squat and ready on the stove. She waited at the kitchen door, bidding him to enter first. As he passed her she felt a fever, as though she had for the moment drawn too close to a flame. He stood by her father's chair and she stepped back, struck, as though seeing a specter, for no one had dared take Edward Dickinson's place at the table since his death. A shadow passed over her excitement and she experienced in that moment the same apprehension she had when she entered her father's empty room.

"Did Mary and Abbie accompany you?" she asked uneasily.

"They are visiting with your brother and his family. Lavinia too, of course." He was sitting now and smiled reassuringly at her. "Come sit beside me," he said.

Emily nervously complied.

"Avoiding issues is a foolish thing, Emily. It distorts, magnifies, or worse—disqualifies the obvious."

The words were stern but his voice was tense with tenderness. She made to turn away, and he gently brought her face back toward him and brushed a stray hair from her forehead as he spoke.

"I am a man who is very intense and outspoken in his opinions. Perhaps that makes me unpleasant to some people, but I can follow no other path. I also see no benefit in beating around the bush. I am in love with you." She started to rise, and he reached for her hand. "No, hear me out. I have loved you for years, even while Elizabeth was alive. Whatever others might say, there is no crime committed by man's fantasies or woman's either! The nasty bigotry of narrow minds *can*, however, perpetuate a crime." He was holding her hand tightly in his own and he now rested them both on the hard bare table. "Are you going to allow them to shatter all your desires and hopes and dreams into atoms? And then will you leave them to sweep those dreams beneath the floorboards of this house as if they were dust and spider webs?" He leaned in closer to her, his hand still locked over hers. "You have declared your love for me. I treasure that as I treasure you. We can wait for spring. There is propriety in that. But any longer, Emily, and it would be a damned waste!"

He let go her hand. The fever remained but there no longer was fear or timidity in her honest gaze as he continued.

"I am not as close to autumn as our respective families would like to believe. And you, Emily, are somehow locked in an eternal spring. We have good years before us. Marry me."

It was a moment before she could reply, and her breathing had become uneven. "You must remember," she said finally, her voice soft and hesitant, "how difficult it will be for me to leave this house." She rose and went over to the window. The fading light of the winter day shadowed half her face. "There is Mother," she tried to explain.

"There is also Austin, Sue, and Lavinia," he added for her.

"It would not be fair."

"We can bring your mother to Salem."

Emily did not reply.

"There is only one obstacle to our marriage," he said. "The shadows that walk in this house. The spirit of your father which seems to have inhabited your flesh." He got up from the chair and went to her and turned her to him so that she was out of the shadow. "Self-denial? Is that what you propose? Haven't we denied ourselves too much all ready? Surely the indecision I see in your eyes cannot stem from doubting our love. Nor can it be possible that you could believe that love inexpedient in any way."

"Oh no, Otis, no," she gasped. She leaned against him and rested her head upon his chest. He held her in his arms and both were silent for a time. Finally she was able to draw away and support herself. "It is the past, of course," she began. "I agree, Father could not bear to find me absent. I think about that in considering leaving here. But it would no longer weight my decision. I have been *this* Emily for so long now. At first I suffered loneness. Now it is my most trusted companion."

She walked away and across the room so that there was a distance between them. "I have had much time to think since our last meeting," she continued, her head high, her voice clear. "And especially this week, knowing you might come again." She took a deep breath. "Otis, I am not certain my soul is mine to give. There is a ghost within me, you see. I am haunted just as surely as any house could be."

"Your writing?"

"Only partly."

"My work is at times my mistress. I see no difference and expect no sacrifices from you that I would not submit to myself," he told her. "If you require two lovers— I accept that. What I could not accept is your denial of one to the loss of the other. In the end it would diminish both." He took a step closer to her. "Answer one question, Emily. Do you love me?"

"You know I do!"

"Answer a second question, then. How long have you loved me?"

"Oh, Otis, *ages*—since Boston. No! Before. Since

*always.* I wrote you once—after Boston, after Elizabeth had joined you and I had returned home. I confessed it all then. I have confessed it again only recently. That letter you have received. *Twas my one glory—let it be remembered. I was owned of thee,"* she added softly.

"Marry me, Emily," he asked again and each stepped closer to the other. He was looking down at her, studying the face he so dearly loved.

"I need time," she begged.

"We have little to spare."

Her hand trembled as it rose to her throat and a lost smile wandered across her face.

"I wish I understood completely, Emily. I will try. I promise you that. But if I don't comprehend your indecision, believe me, I do perceive your torment and suffer with you." He held her narrow shoulders between his broad hands. "You must be honest. Are you afraid of married life?" he asked, tenderness and concern in his touch and his expression.

"Not the way you mean."

He stood away from her and then began to pace, pausing as he spoke to make his points. "What we need is time together away from Amherst and away from this house. Propriety be damned! Our lives are at stake. You are more your own woman elsewhere. I saw that in Boston. It is the only answer." He stopped now, studied her for a moment, and then spoke with authority. "I am to preside over a murder case in Springfield in April. That is only three months away. Meet me there. You could stay with Mrs. Holland, or Mrs. Bowles, or with some very dear friends of mine—Henry and Chloe Murray. I will make all arrangements if your decision is *yes.*"

She was taken aback and swayed unsteadily. He did not reach out to support her. It was as though he had decided she must now stand on her own two feet. "May

I send you my answer?" she finally said in a weak voice.

"If you must."

She went over to the window, stared out at the winter scene. "A murder trial!" she exclaimed.

"Quite a controversial one."

"The Kidder brothers."

He was surprised. "I would not dream you would read about such things."

"The Springfield papers have kept me in touch with life. And then, of course, a case like this is so tantalizing to anyone who is a student of family behavior! Twins— and only one guilty and both confessed! How does one prove which one? And for the victim to have been the father of both! When exactly does the trial begin?" She was facing him now and her expression was alive, her eyes dancing.

"The twenty-fourth of April," he replied, his voice filled with hope.

"The only murder case I remember was Dr. Webster's. I think I shall never forget it," she said. "Of course, it was terribly shocking for a professor in the Harvard Medical School to kill another illustrious doctor in a fit of anger! Even here in Amherst the grisly details were devoured daily until the judge condemned Dr. Webster to hang by the neck until dead." She shivered.

"Oh, Otis,—have you ever condemned a man to death?"

"Yes," he admitted.

"It must have been terrible for you."

"It was."

She turned toward the window again and seemed to be studying the distance. "I have the most curious confession to make. When I was in Boston, I went to see his grave—Dr. Webster's—and I placed flowers upon it. I know he was a murderer and that sin should be punished, but that black and dismal tragedy made me feel as compassionate to the guilty as to the victim. How he must have suffered!"

The judge cleared his throat, and then could not help but laugh. "Have you any idea how you are making me suffer now, Emily?" he asked, and walked over to her.

He towered above her, making her feel even smaller than her diminutive size, making her feel once again like the small child who had climbed upon his knee.

"I will go to Springfield, Master," she whispered, and he leaned down and kissed her on the forehead, and then, unable to control his emotions, boldly seized her.

"Emily," he said, his voice shaking. "I shall make you happy. It is my vow."

So far was their vision fixed upon the future, they did not see Abbie and Lavinia pass before the window, stop and stare in abject horror at the lovers locked in embrace, and then hurry to the rear door to interrupt them.

*6*

---

*A*ustin stood resolute and erect before the cold ashes of the sitting-room hearth. He had, without precedent, come unannounced, choosing a time when Lavinia was to be absent. Austin was a man who considered the kitchen a backland, woman's country. He held the squire's gold-handled cane (bequeathed to him as the squire's Bible had been to Emily) and he wore the red wig he had recently acquired and which gave him his only small resemblance to their father. When he had been younger, Austin had dyed his naturally fair hair the same russet-red of Edward Dickinson's.

Yet, Austin did present an indomitable figure, his eyes unflinching, his face stern, his mouth set grimly and his shoulders steeled, but his father had eyes with double depths and a gaze of righteous sureness that could accuse with rigid calm. Though it was clear that Austin considered himself a figure of authority, he lacked the older man's powerful presence. Somehow, one could always penetrate Austin's pathetic disguise and find the robust youth dressed in ill-fitting clothes imitating a state of being he could only hope someday to achieve.

He was now a man past middle age, and as Emily listened to him, she could not help but yearn that the distance of years could dissolve. She had loved Austin very much when they were young. It seemed to her that *her* Austin had been lost somewhere on a battlefield in the Great War and that this severe-looking middle-aged man lecturing her was a stranger.

"I do not believe that you are aware of the consequences of some of your actions," he said as he pressed the tip of the cane harshly into the ossified hair of the lion rug. The bone white hide showed through, and Emily was at once fascinated and repelled by it. "I am not suggesting a lack of *wit*, dear sister, but rather an unworldliness due to the sheltered, protected life Father and I always secured for you. Frankly, I have been shocked at your behavior in respect to Judge Lord, and in view of my position in the matter."

Emily drew her shawl closer about her shoulders, remaining silent.

"I suppose your excess of temperament is caused by your sex," he commented dryly as he paced back and forth. "It is evident in Sue, as well. But *you* are a Dickinson. That makes a substantial difference."

"Does it?" Emily questioned sharply.

"Of course it does!"

"If you will bear with my excess of temperament, dear brother, I do not agree. A Dickinson does not come neatly packaged like your tobacco. A Dickinson can be man or woman, straight or bending."

He paused and stared at her. "Emily, it is my duty as Father's representative, and as your brother, to tell you that I disapprove of Judge Lord."

"I have come to the unpleasant conclusion, Austin, that you would disapprove of any man who might be interested in me."

"Ridiculous! I shan't bore you with the past, but I will ask you to recall your condition on your return from Boston. Don't think we did not surmise that Otis Lord was at the root of your misery. Have you so little pride that you could openly invite such humiliation again?"

"I don't care to discuss this any further with you, Austin," she managed, the words clipped and painfully formed. Austin cleared his throat in reprimand and she was forced to turn aside in order to control her rising anger.

"He was a married man. His actions were inexcusable. And his pretense at being Father's friend shocking," Austin stated flatly.

She turned sharply back to face him. "Say no more, Austin," fire in her voice.

"Where is your pride, Emily?"

He towered over her as her father had, but that did not intimidate her as she stood before him. "You have refused Otis Lord's petition," she said, coolly and with composure, studying him closely, not pleased with what she found, her confidence growing. "But I don't know what I am going to do yet, Austin. One thing, however, is certain. Your disapproval will not alter my decision."

Austin stiffened. "It is difficult for me to say this to you, Emily, but I would feel that it was a dereliction of duty on my part to continue your allowance if your decision should be a wrong one."

"Wrong, Austin? Or simply not in accord with your own?"

"I only pray the Lord leads you up the right path," he replied.

The smile could not be repressed. "Indeed, I hope that, as well," she said.

He went past her, out into the hallway, and took his cloak and hat from the same peg that had held his father's. He did not kiss her farewell, and though she followed him, he bid her come no closer and so expose herself to drafts. Then, nodding his head as though in dismissal, he opened the rear door and was gone.

Emily spun around in the hallway. She breathed so deeply it pained her, and then she slowly exhaled. No genie appeared. She walked deep into the house, through the dining room to the small glass conservatory. The cold air of the bitter afternoon frosted the glass and curtained the windows. She tolerated no ordinary plants in this room, and so the white shelves which ran around it were lined with pots of fern and purple heliotrope and Daphne odora, and the majestic Cape Jasmine. Oxalis hung from baskets dripping incense and a Ressurection Calli stood saintly in a corner.

She never allowed the conservatory stove to die in winter or in spring, and so this room knew no season, felt no other presence but nature's. She came here often when she had a decision to make.

Austin could never separate himself from the past and enter a new world. Emily felt certain of this. She had to ask herself the question. *Could she? Yes,* her heart told her, *yes, yes!* What could Austin do about that? What would her father have done? She could see him as plainly this moment as she had just seen Austin. He was dressed in black broadcloth and carried his gold-handled cane.

She sat down on a small stool and spread her hands to the warmth of the stove. She recalled how she felt as she had walked beside her father through the town and from the side of her eye noticed that he would tip his glossy beaver hat as he passed the townspeople, never acknowledging them otherwise. She could still smell the musty church odors as he sat aloof on the pew beside her, listening with such intensity to the sermons that deep crevices would form between his piercing eyes. There had been an aura of *old* England about him and she had been able to see that the farmers and the townspeople sitting in their rough homespuns in near pews felt the difference. He seldom spoke, but the people looked at him with more pious eyes than they looked at the preacher. To them—as to herself—he had represented the Puritan ideal of formal authority, probity, and the will for righteous order.

What would her father have said if she had told him she was contemplating meeting Otis Lord in Springfield? It seemed outrageous, but she knew, even at her age, she could not have told him anything of the sort. Nor would he have approved, any more than Austin, any man who wanted her to leave *his* home.

She wondered if he was fully aware of what he had been doing, if he had set about when she was very young to preserve her for himself. Admittedly he had been jealous of any intruders. He had not liked her to entertain friends or receive letters, or to read any book but the Bible—unless it expounded his own philosophies. Only recently had she come to understand that one reason for his not objecting when she did not join the church was that he preferred that she look to him for guidance and for trust.

She tucked her hands into her lap, wishing she could as easily dispose of her thoughts. But she could not, and their weight caused her to sigh deeply. She was waging an important battle with herself. She knew somehow that her father's picture of an evil world had been painted with design. She had great insight into the truth before he died, but formality, love, and duty had forced her to keep her silence. Poems were hidden. True thoughts were never outwardly expressed.

The confrontation with Austin had been a very positive thing. In a way it had been a dual confrontation, as though Edward Dickinson had stood by his son's side, as if she had confronted them both. Emily smiled to herself.

She rose unsteadily to her feet. To join Otis in Springfield she would first have to be sure she could leave this house. It had been many, many years since she had gone past the front door. Sudden excitement flushed her face and she ran from the conservatory, taking only her shawl and holding it tightly about her as she opened the door and stepped out into the afternoon cold. For an anguished moment she thought she might be forced to turn back. She paused, shivering, afraid to breathe the bitter air. What was only a moment seemed endless. Finally she lowered her head and pressed her chin in close to her chest, and her hands beneath her arms, tight to her body, she walked on, continuing down the path to the granite steps that would take her off Dickinson land and onto the main street.

There she stopped and slowly raised her head and looked before her. The street was deserted, not even a carriage in sight. She stood there laughing, yet crying softly, her heartbeat quickening, warmth returning.

*Oh, Salem, my darling Salem,* she sang to herself before turning and walking briskly up the path and inside the house.

# 7

*V*innie was overflowing with
gossip when she arrived not more than ten minutes later.
As they worked side by side in the kitchen, Emily appeared to be listening, but Vinnie sensed something
unusual. "Emily, what is it?" she finally asked. Emily
dismissed her concern with a gesture. "Austin was
here!" Vinnie pressed.

"Yes, Austin was here."

"What did he say to you?"

"I believe that is between Austin and myself."

Vinnie stepped back, injured. "It was about Otis
Lord, I know it was."

"If you knew, why did you ask?"

"See! See? Oh, Emily, that man is even making you
hostile to me. *Me!* It is simply too upsetting." She sank
dejectedly into a chair. "Father would turn in his grave"
was her final thrust.

"I'll take Mother's tray to her," Emily said, ignoring
Vinnie's brooding glance as she passed her.

Vinnie waited for a long time, but Emily did not
return. She had gone to her room after tending their

mother. Vinnie could hear her pacing the hard floor. Timidly Vinnie knocked on the door and asked her to come down to dinner.

"Shortly," Emily said through the closed door. But she remained in her room.

Vinnie did not know what to make of it. She ate by herself and then went to her own room to consider what should be done. She collapsed into the chair at her dressing table. A curl fell onto her forehead and she brushed it back with a coquettish gesture. Her hand trembled. She was frightened and she knew it. Emily would not, *could not* leave. She sat back, startled, not knowing what had put that thought in her head. Nothing had been said about Emily's going away. And yet, somehow, she suspected that was the truth.

She rearranged all the oddments on the table before her. In the end she found she had replaced them to their original position. Life was like that. She understood that, and Emily must as well.

She smiled uneasily at herself in the looking glass. She had, of course, always been the pretty one. Father had taught her honesty, and so she could not lie to herself. She was still the pretty one. Yet Emily was the sun and had always radiantly been so. She had never been as clever with her mind or her hands as Emily had. She could not write a proper letter. She had never been able to converse with her father's friends. She simply did not understand politics or law. It all sounded such a mumbo-jumbo. Even the responsibility of having to prepare a meal by herself terrified her, and the thought that she might be left alone to tend Austin's children for as short a time as minutes unstrung her.

If it had not been so out of the question she might once have enjoyed becoming an actress. She had thought about it when she was younger. There had been beaux, especially Jack. But she did not like to think about that. Anyway, the idea of marriage had always unsettled her. She would have been expected to do all the things she was so bad at doing. And to have borne children—she was certain that would have been quite impossible. Such tests of nature were truly unthinkable. Just to contemplate sleeping with a man, had it even been Jack (in fact, emphatically had it been Jack), presented her with a great wave of pain.

She could never imagine her father undressed. Nor Austin either. Whenever she closed her eyes and brought them to mind, she saw them both in their shiny black broadcloths, holding tight that gold-handled cane. All her tutors had been like that, with the firmly gripped ruler ready always as an instrument of justice and punishment. When they had been girls, Emily had been able to stand up to anyone, even to Miss Lyon, who was the headmistress at Mt. Holyoke Seminary. Miss Lyon had harassed Emily all the time because she was not a professing Christian. And because she was the only student bold enough to rise before her terrifying austerity. Perhaps her father had been right in withdrawing Emily early one year and taking her to Boston, detaining her so long that she could not return to Mt. Holyoke. The truth was, Vinnie would not have minded had it been her, except that then her father would have been her tutor as he had been Emily's.

Vinnie ran her hand over her face. The skin was soft and smooth. That pleased her. It would, she felt, still please Jack. She pinched her cheeks and watched the pinkness grow. She had the look of an amused or defiant child.

"I mustn't dwell on these things," she reminded herself, and turning her glance away, idly tapped her fingers on the table. But no amount of self-willing seemed to help. She began nervously to pace her lavender bedroom, the delicate violets on the wallpaper her aimless point of concentration. A disturbing thought crossed her mind and she stopped sharply.

The judge had such an *earthiness* about him. A woman knew immediately what was pressing forward in his mind, and Vinnie's sensibilities were offended that Emily did not. Worse yet, that she was not repelled. It disrupted the harmony between them, for if she was wrong about Emily, then it meant she truly did not know her. How could she defend her life of dedication to her sister or her sacrifice of Jack's love, if that were true?

Unable to stand the closeness of her room, she left it and started to the staircase. Emily's door opened and Emily stood in her pathway. "Oh, Vinnie, how lucky you are dressed."

"It's still early," Vinnie managed.

"Yes, I was thinking that, and wondering if you were about, if you might not welcome an evening walk to Sue's." She held out an envelope. "Sue promised to read this for me."

Vinnie knew that Emily was in the habit of sending Sue poems for comment. It had been a matter of great irritation to Vinnie. Emily respected Sue's judgment and often acknowledged that she was the only intellectual member of the family. It set Sue apart. It meant things passed between Emily and Sue that Vinnie knew nothing about.

"Can't it wait until morning?" she asked.

"Yes, of course." Emily withdrew her hand and took a step forward.

"Actually, I think I might like a bit of air," Vinnie said. She took the envelope from Emily and hurried downstairs with it. As she fastened her cloak she watched Emily, now in the kitchen, putting up a kettle and humming as she did so.

Seeing Sue now seemed to Vinnie an important mission. It would be difficult to admit to Sue that she needed her help, that *they* required it, but fact was fact. Sue *was* the only member of the family whom Emily might listen to. *Might*.

She walked as fast as she could down the path to Austin's house. Memories, like sudden flashes of fire, rose in her to fight the cold. *Their father's return from the Whig Convention in '52!* It had been held in Baltimore, and Judge Lord had also attended and had stopped in Amherst with their father on his return before continuing on to Salem. Emily had been twenty-two then and the judge many years her senior. Vinnie, as she sat primly working at her sewing that day, had been aware of the same thing in Emily she had recalled moments before. There was a strong attraction between Otis Lord and Emily, and he a married man! It was a good thing that their father had observed nothing. *Or was it?*

After that, Vinnie was conscious that Emily was different when the judge came to visit. Once she spoke about it to her.

"Well," Emily had replied slowly, "there is so much in his face—so much of the outer world. When I look at him it is as though I have tasted life—and oh, Vinnie, it seems such a vast morsel!"

They never spoke of love, but still Vinnie sensed it, and more—sensed the depth of that emotion. Vinnie could never confide such a thought to a living soul, but she suspected that Emily's renunciation of the world, her white robes, had to do with Otis Lord.

It seemed so obvious to Vinnie, she was constantly in fear that her father and the town might guess the truth. People always inquired about Emily's odd behavior, and whenever she could do so delicately, she would hint that Emily's love for a man of the cloth was responsible, hoping that no one would suspect Otis Lord, knowing full well that her loyalty to Emily was so accepted, no one could consider her guilty of duplicity.

Only Sue sneered at this cover-up and countered with the very basic flaw in it. Emily had never joined the church, refusing steadfastly to do so even after all the others in the family had. *If she were so bound to a man of cloth, would not that have been her first step to a spiritual union?* Sue had questioned, all the time giving the impression that she knew more than Vinnie.

Wasn't it just like Sue to contend that the very reason Emily had not joined the church was because her heart was outside the doctrines and that her union, though unconsummated, was decidedly not spiritual in that case! What was Sue insinuating?

Vinnie shuddered and tried to make the image disappear. She had passed the hedge dividing the two houses and was on her way up the walk to Austin's front door. She knew he was not at home, but at a meeting at the College, and was glad of it.

Little golden-haired Gilbert greeted her and then she was besieged by Martha and Ted. The high pitch of the children's voices grated on Vinnie's nerves and she was thankful when Sue came in from the kitchen.

Vinnie breathed a sigh of relief when Sue told the children they must go right to bed. She grasped the collar of her cloak and drew it tighter about her neck, as though suddenly overtaken by a chill.

"Whatever is it, Vinnie?" Sue asked with alarm, the children's voices now in another part of the house.

Vinnie put aside all her mistrust of Sue. This was an emergency and she desperately needed her assistance. "Oh, Sue," she cried. "It's that man! I am afraid that

Emily might go away with him!" She flung herself into her sister-in-law's arms and wept against her maternal chest. "We must stop her, Sue, we *must*," she whimpered.

There was a moment of tenseness, and then Sue stroked Vinnie's head, and Vinnie caught her breath and sighed.

## 8

---

*E*mily pulled the veil down over her face. The disguise was complete. She preened before the mirror and smiled diffidently at herself. She was dressed in mourning, and the theatricality of it pleased her. Though she had promised Otis to come to him *in white*, to wear white on the streets of Amherst, or Springfield, without the chance of being recognized was impossible.

She dressed in darkness for fear Vinnie might be wakened by the trailings of light from beneath her door. Vinnie could not have stopped her but might have insisted upon accompanying her. That was unthinkable, the same as placing a lion in her own pathway! Therefore, preparations for the trip had to be kept secret.

Discreet arrangements had been made by Otis with his good friend Henry Murray and his wife. She was to be their guest in Springfield. The two men were bound by a friendship that had begun in college at Amherst, and continued through their first employment with Henry Murray's father in his Springfield law firm, remaining steadfast until this day. Emily was quite confident, therefore, that the Murrays could be depended upon in the matter of discretion.

The sky was now awash with early-morning gray. It was past six. If things went as planned, the 7:02 would carry her to Springfield.

She opened the door cautiously and studied the corridor before stepping into it. It was silent and the morning light did not penetrate its dark interior. Walking on padded feet, and with an imbred animal stealthiness, Emily recalled the many times she had slipped along this hallway in the same hushed manner to stand concealed behind the door separating the front parlor from the sitting room, to enable her to listen to the words of her father's guests—or Vinnie's—unseen, unheard, the unsuspected observer. So much of her life had been hidden that it no longer seemed strange for her to walk through darkened corridors.

Standing in the center hallway she listened to the house breathe. Her head was cocked so that an intruder might believe her ear was pressed to a pulsebeat. Finally satisfied that Vinnie and her mother were still sleeping, Emily went into the kitchen. She had written Vinnie a letter telling her that she was going to Springfield for a week's holiday, and she placed it now on the wood table. She turned to leave, but habit held her back. Sighing deeply, she fed wood to the stove, lighted it, and pumping enough water for morning coffee, set the ready kettle by the fire.

Immediately upon leaving the house, Emily lowered the black veil. It distorted her vision, but she was comforted to know that if she could barely see beyond the veil, passers-by could not see behind it.

She hesitated at the granite steps, looking across the road to the open fields and purple hills beyond. Then, resolutely turning her fine brown eyes right, she looked down Main Street. There were others on the road and a carriage before the smithy's shop. Her heart beat very quickly. So long a time had passed since she had walked up that street. Catching her breath, she realized with shock and bewilderment and perhaps a tinge of disbelief that she was terrified. No Stone Age woman seeing the civilized world for the first time could have felt more disoriented.

The carriage finally pulled away from the curb, and clutching the collar on her cape, and gathering her wits and her courage, she stepped down and onto the walk. Standing thus for several seconds, poised, feeling very small, a child, in fact, she experienced her first and only doubt. Behind her another carriage rattled on the road, its *clack-clack* drawing ominously close. She hesitated, almost turning to dart back into the house. Shame overcame her, and then anger. She flung herself forward and marched firmly away from the squire's house and up the road to the station.

This life, this protective cloak she had been wrapped in for so many years, would, if she continued her resolve, no longer engulf her. A ghost of a smile slipped gently across her face. She crossed the road to avoid passing even remotely close to Austin's, and this action gave her further courage. April promise was in the fresh morning air, and light so crystal-clear that she felt her spirits lift. From behind her widow's veil her eyes flashed brazenly.

A fire burned within the smithy's shop and horses' neighs and workmen's gusty voices assailed her. With an incredible daring she paused and looked within. The men glanced up, perhaps sensing her presence or noting her black shadow on the sunlit ground. They were startled to see her. The younger man scrambled to his feet and stepped back with fear. It was her widow's dress, she

thought, those waves of black surrounding and concealing her.

"Death has come for his chariot!" he cried out.

"Nonsense," cautioned the older man, yet he did not
move. "Can I help you, ma'am?" he asked, not recogniz-
ing Emily, though as a young man he had seen and
spoken to her often.

"I'm looking for the station," Emily replied, knowing full well where it was but at a loss as to what else to
answer.

"The other side of the square. Impossible to miss it.
You're wanting the seven-oh-two, I guess." Smiling awkwardly, he rose from his crouched position at the forge.
He was deeply uncomfortable facing a woman in mourning even at a distance of thirty feet, and he speculated
that she was either going to meet the train and therefore
a coffin, or was boarding it to travel to a funeral. Someone's visiting relation, he guessed, and made a mental
note that he would ask around and find out who she
might be.

"Perhaps my son could escort you," he suggested.

The son hung back in the shadow, and Emily de-
clined the offer, much to the young man's relief. She
moved light-heartedly back onto the street and stepped
briskly forward. The disguise had worked!

The ticket was secure in her pocket. The judge had
purchased and sent it to her so that she would not have
to speak to the ticket man, but at this moment Emily felt
she could have managed that confrontation as well.

There was a ten-minute wait for the train's arrival.
Standing to one side of the platform, she kept her gaze
high, as though watching a bird fly off into the horizon.
Her mind was filled with many memories. She recalled
trips taken years before. Boston—where she had known
her first awakening and her most soul-searing disap-

pointment. Now here she was, decades having passed, waiting for the train to deliver her into Otis Lord's care. In less than two hours, time would continue to tick off the minutes as though the intervening moments had not existed. As if those years had been a dream, another life.

The train was aproaching, drew closer, the sound filling her head as it roared into the station. She had to turn her head away so violent was the rush of air. It shivered, silenced, halted.

She boarded the nearest car and sat in a rear seat. Placing her small handbag on the empty seat beside her to discourage future occupancy, Emily leaned back and closed her eyes.

The train jolted forward. Springfield and Otis Lord waited.

# Springfield

*O*tis Lord loved Emily as he had never loved another woman in his life. Always a passionate man, she awakened the sexual fantasies he had dreamed of as a young man. He could see her curled up and sleeping at his feet, a small child needing protection against the cold night; her hair loosened and her lips trembling as she breathed a troubled sleep. A desire to protect and possess her would then come sharply upon him and his heart would beat as if he had been running a mile. He would bend over her and lift her in his arms, her look on awakening filled with a wildness of innocence as she clung to him without shock or fear, with, instead, a joyous eagerness. There was always a mist at this point in his reverie and it would thicken as he walked with her, so that all around them was obscure. They were visitors to another world. And always the dream—for such it was—ended there.

At his age such fantasies were embarrassing, and their lack of fulfillment most disturbing, but Otis Lord's sense of irony never deserted him. Here he was, desiring to possess innocence and at the same time planning deliberately to betray it.

He sat alone in his hotel room, having just completed a solitary breakfast. A fire burned in the grate. It was early morning and the trial for which he had come to Springfield would begin the following day. He had arrived early to ready everything for Emily's visit and to insure for the two of them the greatest privacy so that they might have a fair chance to know each other, to learn of each other's frailties as well as attributes.

He was far too honest not to confess to himself, at least, that he had ordered things in such a way that the latter would outshine the former. Emily would be observing him apart from the women in his household, watching him daily as he reigned omnisciently in his courtroom, and she would be stopping with his friends, hearing his side to every incident. But though the picture might be one-sided, there was no doubt that Emily needed and loved him and that he needed and loved Emily. Every consideration must, therefore, be given (or taken) to bring their situation to a happy conclusion.

What did disturb him was that he had taken rooms at the Messassoit. Custom would have decreed another course. Habit would have housed him with friends, and he had many in Springfield, though none as close as the Murray family. He did not rationalize the action to himself. He had secured rooms so that he and Emily would have, if she were receptive, a place where they could be alone. It could well appear that he was compromising Emily in such an action, even if Emily never visited him. He was aware of this and considered it a calculated risk, but it had not deterred him.

Right now she was on her way to him. Though he would have liked to meet her train, that would cause too much speculation. Alternate arrangements had been made for Mrs. Murray to meet Emily and for the two ladies to go directly to the Murray house. He was slightly uneasy over Emily's reaction to the Murray family. He had informed her that they were Jewish and the information had not colored her decision to stop with them and so support his desires. But remembering now Elizabeth's cold attitude to his dear friends, he was vaguely concerned. Vaguely, because he thought he knew Emily well enough to dismiss any concern in the matter. But then, and of course, this was exactly the point—how well did any man know any woman?

He turned his thoughts to the Kidder case, which, though fraught with problems, was much safer ground. On the night of June 7, 1881, Dwight Kidder was seen running in a distraught manner from the Carew Street home of his invalid and elderly father. Only moments later the servant girl, Maud Hagarty, entered Old Man Kidder's room after hearing scuffling sounds. She found the senior Kidder lying face down on the floor by the side of his bed (an unusual circumstance, since it was believed the man could not have arisen from his bed without assistance). Blood gushed from a wound in his shoulder, but there was a pool of blood beneath him which indicated a further and more serious wound must have been inflicted in his chest. The Hagarty woman ran to fetch Dr. Crane, a friend and neighbor. The doctor ascertained that the man had been shot dead and thereupon went for the medical examiner, who in turn notified the police.

Dwight Kidder had been apprehended within twenty-four hours and Nathanial Leonard was engaged as his counsel. Until this moment and although the crime of patricide was certainly shocking, the case appeared to be following a circumscribed course. But then the prisoner, pleading his innocence, was arraigned. At the arraignment the young woman who had identified as Dwight Kidder the man she had seen running from the

Carew Street house, was called as witness, and was asked to point to the man she saw that night. She directed her attention to the young man seated beside the defense counsel.

"That's himself," she cried, "that's Dwight Kidder."

"Are you unequivocally certain?" Mr. Leonard inquired.

"I be."

At that moment a man stood at the rear of the courtroom.

"Your honor," he called out.

All eyes turned to him with shock, for in every aspect the man appeared to be the very image of Dwight Kidder, and indeed he was, for this man was Charles Kidder, Dwight's identical twin.

"Come forward," the judge ordered.

Charles Kidder walked up the aisle of the hushed courtroom and stood by his brother's side.

"Now," Mr. Leonard asked the girl, "can you still positively identify this man as Dwight Kidder."

The witness was obviously taken aback. "I can positively state it to be one 'tother, sir."

To the courtroom's dismay, *both* men were thereupon arraigned for trial on charges of murder and conspiracy. So it would be a case that would receive unusual publicity and might very well set a legal precedent. Attorney General Waterman was conducting the prosecution himself and was setting forth the claim that both men, Charles and Dwight Kidder, had conspired to murder their father, and by confusing witnesses, as they had done when they were children as a prank, had in a most heinous manner believed they had committed the perfect crime.

Otis Lord sighed deeply. It would not be an easy case. The fire was burning low but he did not feed it another log. Instead, aware that he had time to kill, he donned his coat and left the hotel and began what he anticipated as a leisurely stroll to the Murray house. But after a very short while he felt cold and chilled to the marrow, and raised his stick to a passing hansom.

The driver stopped but did not step down to help his fare inside. The judge gave the man a look of reprimand and then opened the door himself. For a moment he felt weary, as though the effort was too much for him. Then, inside, he leaned gratefully back against the worn leather and rested.

His case with Emily, he feared, also might not be an easy one. He pulled his greatcoat closer about him and inhaled the musty air inside the cab. *Emily . . . Emily.*

*T*he hansom drew up at the corner of Maple and Temple streets and behind another cab. As the judge stepped quickly down from his vehicle he caught a glimpse of a woman in mourning, and for a moment was very uneasy. Could someone close to the Murray family have died and he not notified? He instantly removed his hat and stepped forward with a slight bow. The woman glanced up at him through her veil and smiled.

"Emily!" he exclaimed.

She laughed. "Even you didn't recognize me!"

Chloe Murray in all her amplitude heaved mightily as she stepped from the cab to the sidewalk. "Wheelchairs and widow's weeds," she said. "Guaranteed to speed service. Miss Dickinson is very clever."

The judge's driver set his whip in the stand beside his seat, and jumping down and to the judge's side, held out a chilblained hand. "Please tend to your co-worker as well," the judge said as he paid the man generously.

The cabby grinned and walked away and over to the first hansom, where the two men acknowledged each other and stood watching the judge and the ladies as they started up the stone walk to the Murray house.

The house was in every respect stately and gracious and not in the least foreboding. It was set well back on the crest of a soft rise. Early roses lined the walk to the wide front veranda with its curved and elegant railings shaded by a giant chestnut tree. Three wholesome, apple-cheeked children stood crowded together in the open doorway to the house. Even at a distance one could sense their high spirits and guess as well that a restraining hand was not far away.

The waiting youngsters could contain themselves no longer, and pulling suddenly free from the invisible strings that had been holding them back, bounded down the steps, raced down the walk, and then, halting just a few feet in front of their mother and in her pathway, stood with some embarrassment and awkwardness. There were two girls and a boy. The boy was youngest —about four. He had startling red hair and eyes that squinted like a cat's.

"Children, children!" Chloe chided. She pushed the boy forward. "You know Judge Lord, Isaiah?"

The judge smiled and extended his hand, but the boy hung back.

"Isaiah, I'm surprised at you," his mother said.

The boy took the judge's hand but never looked him in the eye.

"Hello, Isaiah." Emily smiled, taking the flowers that were tucked in her waist and offering them to the child.

He came directly to her. "They're pretty," he said, nervously accepting them and then running back up the walk and onto the front veranda, where a woman now stood.

The two girls giggled and their mother took each by

the hand. "This is Jerusha." She nodded to the tallest, a dark-haired nine-year-old who looked a lot like her. "And this is Deborah." Deborah curtsied and smiled coquettishly. She had the same coloring as Isaiah and was the beauty in the family, and it was apparent that even at six she was aware of the fact. She held her head high, as beautiful women proud of their looks have always done, and she moved with alarming assurance for so small a child.

The woman who had appeared on the front veranda stepped out of the shadows as Chloe Murray, her children, and her guests drew close. "I apologize for the children's demeanor," she said, but her incredibly hard, lean body never bent, and her dark eyes never wavered.

"It's all right, Miss DePeters," Chloe told her.

Once in the hall, the woman called softly, almost under her breath, "Children," and all three went immediately to her side.

"Lessons," she reminded them and they marched behind her and out of the room.

"I don't know what we would do without Miss De-Peters," Chloe commented. "As you can see, she is part Indian. Her grandmother was the daughter of a missionary and was carried off when she was very small by the Abenakis in Canada. She grew up in their tribe and married one of their young braves. The story goes that her father never gave up trying to get her back, and though she died before he could succeed, her husband and the tribe finally agreed to let him have the first girl of that union. That was Miss DePeters' mother, who was then about ten. They brought her to Deerfield but, shamefully, the citizens never accepted her. A Frenchman fell in love with her, however, and took her back to Canada as his bride. That, of course, was Miss DePeters' father. She had a fine education and is a marvelous governess. The children don't seem to mind learning French grammar if they can also hear Indian tales!"

Chloe Murray suddenly became aware of her role as hostess. "How thoughtless of me! Miss Dickinson must be exhausted!"

"Miss Dickinson is quite the opposite." Emily laughed. "Miss Dickinson is highly exhilarated."

"Agnes, Agnes!" Chloe called. "I don't know where that girl is gone to, but there is a fire in the library and when I find her I'll have her bring coffee there. Oh, and let me take your cloak and bag." She did so, and continued talking. "You know where the library is, Otis. That's where you and Henry have all those women-forbidden talks!"

The judge laughed lightly, took Emily by the arm, and directed her across the large center hall and to a door to the rear. Immediately Chloe was gone, though echoes of her voice still filled the air as she took over the management of her household.

The Murray house was unlike any Emily had ever been in before. It was built in the style of an English town house, and, in fact, Henry Murray's father had brought over a well-known London architect to design it. The house had been completed after the old gentleman's death, but Chloe was not the first woman to occupy and furnish it, for she was Henry's second wife. He had been a widower a good deal older than she when Chloe married him ten years before. His first wife had been of English-German heritage, while Chloe's grandparents had been Russian peasants. Therefore, the house had a distinct dual personality. Regency furniture and French carpets and Venetian mirrors were kinsmen to sampler maps and sturdy rough-hewn benches and cabinets. There was also the touch of the exotic, indicating that Chloe had an active imagination, which substantiated Emily's feeling that she was going to like her hostess very much.

The library contained many Indian relics, some lovely English prints, lots of good books, and comfortable chairs for reading. There was a fire in the hearth and the room was warm and appealing.

"Are you all right, Emily?" the judge asked with concern as Emily sat down by the fireplace and clasped her hands in her lap.

"Yes . . . only . . ." Emily began.

"Only what, Emily?"

"I want to know how long we shall wonder at the future. How early we shall know." It was the kind of cryptic thought that was so much a part of Emily.

"Soon, Emily," he assured her.

She smiled nervously. "I enjoyed the train ride very much. We passed mountains that touched the sky and brooks that sang like bobolinks." She glanced aside. "Where will you be staying?"

"I have rooms at the Messassoit Hotel."

She nodded her head. "And the trial?"

"It begins tomorrow."

"May I come?"

"Yes, of course."

She studied her hands. The judge sat beside her and took them into his own.

"I have been able to think of little else but you," he said.

She turned slightly away from him, though she did not withdraw from his grasp. Finally he released her and at the same time gently drew her head around. She was still wearing the veil and he lifted it, and after studying her face for a long moment, a time so painful to Emily that she closed her eyes, he kissed her on the mouth and then lightly on each of her lowered lids. She opened her eyes and stared at him as he rose and went and stood in front of the fire.

"I love you, Emily. I believe I have said that before, but I cannot see that repeating it could diminish its meaning to you in any way."

Whatever Emily might have answered to that, the judge would never know, for at that moment Agnes entered carrying an elegant silver tray with silver coffee service and three of Chloe Murray's best china cups and saucers. They had been left discreetly alone for a lingering greeting, but their hostess was not ignorant of propriety. As Agnes backed out of the room, Chloe entered.

"Henry wanted me to assure you both that had he not had a case on the docket this morning he would have been here to welcome you," she said as she sat down. Her ebullient façade appeared to have dissolved for a moment and she sat as though mesmerized by the small golden flames that gleamed in the shiny silver of the coffee urn. The fire threw shadows on all three of them. Emily also fire-gazed while the judge studied her. Finally Chloe broke the spell that seemed to be so suddenly cast over them.

"Well," she said, regaining her good humor, "I am a romantic!" There was a glint in her eyes that was not a reflection of the fire, but of her own manufacture. "I was recalling Henry's courtship." She sat in a queenly position as she poured coffee and presented a cup to the judge. "You know, Otis, I was thirty-one when we met, and I truly believed I had been passed by. I was already Aunt Chloe to all the children in the family. I thought I should never have any of my own." Chloe's kindly but plain face glowed with memories. "I looked a bit like a dumpling, I'm afraid, but Henry made me feel like Cleopatra and Helen of Troy all at once." She poured another cup of coffee got up and crossed to where Emily was sitting. "Coffee, Miss Dickinson?"

"Please call me Emily."

Chloe smiled warmly and the two women exchanged glances. *I understand,* Chloe's expression said. Emily took the cup from her hand, never lowering her eyes.

"Thank you," she said. "Thank you very much."

Emily's window on the third floor was large and round like an eye, and was set in a gable. From it she looked down at the magnificent elms, and the manicured lawns, cultivated gardens, and massive chestnut trees of the Murray estate.

Chloe had given her the large third-floor guest room that adjoined the children's theater and playroom, and it had been a wise choice. Chloe, Emily decided, was a very wise woman.

Emily left her door open so that she could see into the children's private world. Marionettes hung from the rafters and Emily noted how many Indian characters there were; apparently Miss DePeters' influence. In Emily's room, the roof sloped above a vast space where a large mahogany bed stood, and came to an angled halt above a long table, once used for dining, now set with paper, pen, and ink for Emily's convenience. The walls were stenciled with flowers, and a vase beside the bed was filled with fresh-cut roses.

There were so many new wonders. She could not believe the two mammoth iron bridges that now spanned the Connecticut River when you entered Springfield, they seemed such a marvel of engineering. Nor the railway services that ran from one end of the city to the other and that Chloe claimed ran every fifteen minutes. Yet, standing at the curious circular window and staring out, Emily thought of the greater wonder that man could not alter nature—could not make the trees bud before they chose or sweep away April winds or suppress the scent of rose and heather.

She turned away, smiling, humming a tune to herself, one she used to sing when she was a girl and would walk with her dog Carlo in her father's apple orchards. She was happy then—and she was happy now. *How strong when weak to recollect, and easy, quite to love,* she thought.

She closed her eyes and could almost see Carlo's shaggy-furred image on the inside of her lids. It seemed she had just returned from Mt. Holyoke, studies behind her and the spring holiday her own, and the future, for there was a glorious future to dream of then—a wonderland of imagining.

She opened her eyes and sat down on the edge of the bed. It was possible to dream again. Emily felt the warm tears course down her cheeks. How long ago had she set aside dreams: hampers and corded boxes and trunks full of them?

Her darling Salem had turned her from their path and now was leading her back, and she was in such a hurry to free them that the very effort flushed her heart with pain.

It turned out to be an exceptionally fine day. The sky was a bright, shiny blue polished by the wind, and the sun streamed from it in arcs of gold. It was still very cold, but inside where Otis Lord and Henry Murray were lunching in the dining room of the Messassoit, that was difficult to believe. The linen was white and gleaming, the silver shining, and the food steaming. Through the high latticed windows, framed in drapes of deep crimson velvet, could be seen the rear private garden of the hotel, with its trees and a rainbow of spring flowers. The firelit dining room was warm and pleasant and there was such a pervasive feeling of security that one would naturally believe all the diners would have felt snug and would be experiencing emotions of joy and delight. But at the small and semi-private table in the farthest corner of the room, closest to the garden windows, the two men exchanged troubled glances.

They had known each other since boyhood, and the familiarity between them was so strong that there was very little need to explain themselves or to try to disguise their feelings. The years had proved that they could trust each other, and experience had demonstrated that each would allow and respect differences of opinion. It was curious that in the relationship, though the judge maintained the most imposing appearance and though his rank and notoriety and esteem made him the apparent leader, it was, in fact, Henry who was the spearhead of the two.

The relationship had begun that way when they had been at school together in Amherst. Henry had been the *old fellow*, a year ahead in school, and the younger Otis Lord had come from a distance, knowing no one in the area. The friendship was maintained on the same keel when Otis, the graduate law student, became a clerk in the firm owned by Henry's father. Then it was Henry who went into private practice first, and Henry who married first, and Henry who traveled to Europe when the judge never left the eastern United States, and Henry whose first wife died years before Elizabeth, and Henry who had married, afterward, a woman much younger than himself.

Outside appearances were extravagantly deceptive, for the unremarkable physiognomy and stature of Henry Murray masked a man of varied experience, intense sensitivity, sharp powers of observation, and a quick and intelligent mind that had made him head of his class at Amherst and the most successful lawyer in Springfield.

The two men had finished a meal of stew simmering in hot gravy and devoured the mound of warm biscuits with fresh-churned sweet butter. Henry had ordered a superb wine and the bottle was nearly drained.

Otis leaned across the table, his brow furrowed. "I am concerned, very much concerned. This case is no ordinary murder trial." He straightened, sat up stiffly.

"There is the possibility that either party could exploit it for its own political gain because of the armament issue," he muttered. "I know his lawyer, Nathanial Leonard, well. He is bound to make a point of it. Albert Kidder had business connections with Smith and Wesson. His son has already made a statement to the press that he abhorred the manufacture of firearms. Leonard has set the scene."

"It's not like you to back away from a case just because it promises to be difficult," Henry chided.

"Exploitation," his friend exploded, "it angers and disgusts me!" He hit the table with his fist and several diners turned to look at him and the waiter cleared his throat in warning. Otis Lord lowered his voice, but the anger, the fury seemed, in fact, to build in the very hoarseness of his tone. "Leonard is after political office, and firearms will be his platform. And the attorney general is fighting like Satan to hang onto his position. The Kidder trial is going to be used by both parties, mark my words. This is not going to be a legal trial, but a political ball game. And these boys—these accused young men whose lives hang in the balance—they are to be used, Henry, *used* like tools! It infuriates me!"

"All the more reason for you to make certain that justice sits high in that courtroom," Henry insisted.

Otis relaxed slightly, his voice taking on a more normal tone. "I'm not an ambitious man, Henry. Never have been." He paused, studying his friend's reactions, "The Republicans are applying pressure on me again," he said.

"Are you still disinterested in running?"

"Totally. But suppose, Henry, suppose my final decision in that courtroom supports the Republican platform. What will the press make of that?"

"Does that worry you?"

"I am afraid it does," he admitted.

"Well, Otis, sometimes it occurs in life that an unambitious man driven by the extremity of circumstance must choose a side. Now, if your decision at the end of this trial abets either party, I can see no other alternative than for you to stand behind that decision no matter what the outcome. Stepping down, allowing another man to replace you—perhaps a man less implacable than you—would only defeat your own sense of rightness. No, Otis. Think about it. You *must* sit in that courtroom." He signaled the waiter. "Brandy," he ordered, and looking at his friend for agreement, added, "Two."

The men sat quietly until the waiter returned with the brandy. "I do want to thank you for your graciousness toward Emily," Otis said sincerely, warming the brandy glass between his hands.

Henry did not answer right away. He was studying his friend's face, looking for more than he knew the other man wanted to reveal. "You may not be an ambitious man, Otis, but you are an adventurer and a romantic. There is no turning back for you now, old man. Lovers are as plentiful as blackberries in season when a girl is nineteen. At Miss Dickinson's age a man cannot declare himself and then have a change of heart."

"I have no dream of happiness other than to spend my remaining years with Emily by my side," he replied without hesitation.

The men parted with lingering camaraderie. Otis returned to his rooms and carefully went over various papers and documents. The truth was, the briefs did not need to be tended with such immediacy, or on such a beautiful crisp afternoon, but he could not subdue the anxiety that the luncheon talk had raised in him.

# 12

$\mathcal{L}$ater in the afternoon he returned to the Murrays' with a hired hansom and a plan to take Emily on a tour of the city. But the day was so lovely that he directed the driver to the countryside instead. Emily still wore her widow's garb, but as soon as she stepped into the cab, she removed her veil, holding it in her lap lovingly and as though it were a rare black butterfly. He sat very close to her, but she did not turn to look at him; instead she studied the sheer cloth pressed between her fingers. He was silent, and she was grateful for that. It gave her time to erase the questions that had so painfully etched themselves on her thoughts since he had left her early that morning. At the moment she was proposing names to herself for the veiled illusionary insect she held. The *Ethiopian Spread-Wing* was all she could conjure, and the inanity of it made her smile.

"Good. You are cheering up."

She raised her downcast eyes to meet his. He smiled to reassure her, but he felt awkward, not in control of the situation. Her presence so close beside him filled the narrow confines of the interior of the cab and nearly overpowered him, and to calm himself, Otis turned away from her and looked out the window.

The cab moved smoothly over the brick roads in the central sector of the city. Then it crossed the south-end bridge, kept to the road bordering the riverbank in Agawam and to the junction of Agawam Street. They were headed toward the old covered bridge which would take them to a few less-frequented country lanes. On the way they had passed the huge Smith and Wesson Works, where small arms were manufactured and sent all over the world. By the river stood the imposing Watson Car Company Works, where railway cars were made and shipped as far as Egypt. Springfield was quickly industrializing and it made Judge Lord curiously sad to see it, for he believed manufacture brought with it labor problems, and health problems, and finally, increasing criminal problems.

As they drove noisily over the planks of the covered bridge he gained courage to glance at Emily. She was sitting upright and she was smiling softly to herself. He watched her, all other thoughts erased at sight of her. It was curious how childlike she could seem even in the high-collared black dress. And how gracefully she held her head. She reached up to loosen her collar, and as she did, her eyes again met his. His smile was now unguarded.

"Could we stop awhile and walk?" she asked.

The judge ordered the driver to halt at the far end of the first country lane they reached. They got out of the carriage, and Emily led the way quickly, as though this was a walk she took daily and knew inch by inch. He followed a few feet behind her, laughing as he puffed along. She came to a section of ground that sloped down, and waited for him. He thought she wanted him to help her down, but he was wrong. She went before him, sure-footed as a doe.

They came to a small clear-watered brook in a narrow ravine, bordered with rocks and brambles. A field of lilac trees budded above the green slope that rose from the far side of the brook—a distance of no more than fifteen feet. The spot she had found was completely private.

Removing his cloak, he spread it out on a small smooth section of the downslope, then helped Emily ease herself to the ground. Once there, she grasped her knees and leaned forward, her head turned slightly away from him. "I must explain myself to you," she said. "I know all women present problems of understanding to men, and I know my own queerness—"

"Emily—"

"No. It is quite all right. My queerness," she continued without any inflection upon the word, as though she were saying my *hair* or my *eyes*, "further complicates understanding." She was staring across the brook and at the lilac trees. "I sincerely believe I was like most other girls when I was young and when you first knew me. While I was in boarding school I considered that to be the case. Father, perhaps, was more intense a father than the fathers of the other girls, and my relationship with Mother was vaguer than the other girls with theirs, but I shared their feelings in all other respects. I had the same fears and hopes and misconceptions. I was confident that the one thing quite certain in my future would be marriage. Oh, the Dickinson and Norcross families had the usual sprinkling of maiden aunts. One of them, Vinnie and I used to call the only male on the female side of the family! But none of those ladies, and that one in particular, seemed to bear any likeness to me at all."

She shook her head with a surprising vehemence. "None at all," she said sharply. Then, taking a deep breath and letting it slowly escape her, she went on as though uninterrupted by any spasm of emotion.

"I recall being drawn to you when I was no more than sixteen, and being shocked at my feelings because you were not only much older and more worldly, but also married and a friend of Father's. To think of you in such a fleshlike way, and indeed I did, was shocking and a bit like being drawn sexually to one's father, whom one might also set apart as much older, more worldly, and married!"

He reached for her hand, but she pulled it just out of his reach. There was a slight quiver in her lip and a mist in her eye. "Please—so that I may continue," she whispered. It was a moment or two before she was able to do so. "I carried no guilt," she finally said. "I want you to know that. Other girls were infatuated with teachers or ministers, so I recognized my fantasies as not being out of the ordinary no matter how shocking they seemed."

She paused again for a moment and appeared to be scanning the treetops for birds or other flying creatures. "There were young men after that. Several," she added.

"Did they propose marriage?" he asked softly.

"No, but then neither did I encourage them. Father, of course, deemed them all unworthy, as he did Vinnie's Jack." She turned her head and smiled back at him. "Vinnie was very much in love with him, but Father insisted they wait a year, and as Jack had to go South to a post, he left without Vinnie, and in a year's time, met and married a local girl."

"I didn't know that. I am sorry for Vinnie," he said honestly.

"Vinnie has never really given up hope. That is, she believes when Jack's wife dies—" She turned aside. "Vinnie at times complicates my life. I love her. Please understand that. But when one leans so heavily, it is most difficult for the other. It won't be easy for Vinnie if ever—" She seemed unable to continue.

This time he took her hand and held it tightly. "We'll work that out," he assured her.

She was squinting because the sun shone directly in her eyes, and she turned away and settled her glance on the turn of the brook just beyond them where the water dashed rythmically against the stones. "I know this is very difficult for you," she said, "but I have felt the need for so long—so terribly, terribly long—to confess—"

"Emily, I want to know all and anything you might honor me by confiding," he told her.

She smiled and nodded her head in appreciation. "I became very aware of my narrowing chances of marriage about the same time that Austin and Sue married." She glanced up at him. "Does it embarrass you for me to speak so frankly?" she asked.

He laughed gently and patted her hand.

"I have known Sue since we were girls, and having her live so close has been a great compensation to me. Sue was the first person who understood my need to write and the only one in the beginning to encourage me. Before I went to Boston to consult a physician about my eye condition, Sue insisted I send my poems to Mr. Higginson. He was such a famous editor and his work did seem in empathy with my own ideas. He kept my poems for a long time, but finally he sent them back— rejected them. That was very difficult for me. I have never been able to submit them since that time. Sue understood that, too, and helped me through that crisis. Before Boston—before I had that fleeting loss of vision —I had what might be called a nervous collapse."

"I guessed that," he told her without censure.

"Perhaps, that was why—after Boston—"

"No, I can't let you take the blame for the results of Boston. It is mine entirely," he insisted.

She closed her eyes for a moment. When she opened them she saw that he had glanced away, perhaps so that she should not feel inhibited. "What I am saying is that Sue was—and perhaps is—a great influence on me. The only other equal influence on my work, at least, was my discovery of Mrs. Browning's works, especially *Aurora Leigh.*" She seemed to be gathering up courage. "And now my greatest confession," she began.

Unlike most confessors she neither bowed her head nor turned to face him. Instead she leaned back and stared up at the azure sky, the moving pattern of a drift of clouds.

"In the beginning, most of my poetry was imitative of Mrs. Browning. I read and reread *Aurora Leigh* and would find a passage that meant a good deal to me and say it in poetry in my own words. The poems were my own, but I always felt I owed too much to Mrs. Browning to publish them. That, of course, was after Mr. Higginson's rejection."

"Emily, I'm shocked. Do you mean to say that after one rejection you gave up?" He was scolding her, not in an unkindly tone, but with warmth and caring.

"I couldn't submit again. I simply couldn't," she repeated, much distressed. "That is how the *secrecy* of my writing began, and I suspect was the beginning of what people called my queerness." She sat up straight and folded her skirt tight around her legs. "I feel in some ways I have sinned regarding Mrs. Browning and my work, and I want you to know that."

"Oh, but you haven't, Emily! I am a man of law, not of the arts, but I am acquainted with enough biography to assure you that most great artists and writers and musicians I have read about patterned themselves after other talents—men and women they admired. What you saw, Emily, was a similarity in the themes and the life of Mrs. Browning with your own. Both of you had such strong fathers. Both of you were left in charge of the home. Both were women striving to be poets. It is understandable. Very understandable." He spoke with great sincerity and assurance.

"Thank you, darling Salem, thank you," she whispered. "And perhaps Mr. Browning's entering Elizabeth Barrett's life when he did gave me hope—and strength," she added.

"I should have done that," he said angrily. "Damn my cowardice!"

She reached out and touched his hand, but for a moment was silent. "Well, by the time I went to Boston for my eyes," she said finally, "I was, of course, past thirty and still a 'maiden.' But by then a miracle had occurred. I considered myself a poet first, above all else. The term *spinster* just did not seem to apply to anyone serious about writing. You were, after all, married in one sense to your craft. But then came the trouble with my eyes. I thought I was going blind. I was suddenly unable to write or read. It was the most desolate time in my life until you reentered it!" She turned to him and held out her hand and he grasped it tightly. "In Boston, with you, I became a woman for the first time in my life. Perhaps a man cannot understand that, nor understand the impact of so late and delayed an awakening. Now it seemed I could become what I was meant to become. And then I received your letter that Elizabeth had joined you and that you could not see me again in Boston."

She hesitated. Then she made a little nervous movement of her head, and finally, like a bird sky-diving, she plunged back into her confession. "I was angry at you, very angry, when I returned home. I didn't know if I hated you or if I loved you. As I told you once before, I wrote you a very long letter which I never had the courage to post. In it I said that my love for you was so immense, it frightened me. And I begged you to take me back. I—" She stopped abruptly, and putting her hand in her pocket, brought forth a crumpled sheet of paper. "I've kept a copy all these years."

"Would you read it to me, Emily?"

So many times had she read the words that she had only to glance at the paper from time to time. *"You send the water over the Dam in my brown eyes,"* she began slowly. *"I've got a cough as big as a thimble—but I don't care for that —I've got a Tomahawk in my side but that don't hurt me much. My master stabs me more.*

*"Won't he come to me—or will he make her seek him—"* She glanced up at him; his face showed the strain of conflicting emotions. *"Oh, how the sailor strains, when his boat is filling— Oh, how the dying tug, till the angel comes. Master—open your life wide, and take me in forever. I will never be tired—I will never be noisy when you want to be still. I will be your best little girl—nobody else will see me, but you —but that is enough— I shall not want any more—and all that Heaven only will disappoint me—will be because it's not so dear—"* She replaced the letter in her pocket.

Otis Lord seized her hand then. "There's no going back, Emily—only forward. Marry me, Emily. Marry me before you leave Springfield. Marry me and we will leave here together." He leaned closer to her, but she had turned her face away and concealed her reaction in shadow. "Don't make us both suffer for the past, Emily. What is done, is done. We committed no crime. Elizabeth had lost my love years before, and that it found its way to you was a miracle, Emily. I bless, not curse, that event."

He stood up and helped her to her feet, she was poised as though about to dart away.

"I cannot do it, not in Springfield. Not so soon," she

cried, but she threw herself against his chest and he held her tightly there, his arms clasped about her narrow shoulders. When she drew away, there were no tears on her cheeks. There was, in fact, as he studied her face, a look of abandon, of nature's child set free.

"My darling Salem," she whispered, and paused long enough to kiss his hand. Then she leaned down and swept up his cloak, and laughing, said gaily, "I want to go somewhere—somewhere sundown cannot find us!"

They rode back to the Murrays', where they were to dine. The cab turned the corner of Maple and into Temple and drew into the driveway. Otis Lord stepped out of the carriage and turning his back to the side door of the house as he helped Emily down, he noted her face fill with surprise, felt her hand grasp his tightly. His heartbeat quickened as he sensed she must be looking over his shoulder and into the face of danger.

Sue Dickinson was standing in the Murray doorway, and the expression on her face would have chilled a blazing desert sun.

## 13

$\mathcal{T}$he two women were ushered into the library and left in privacy.

"Austin agreed to let me come," Sue began immediately and without any preamble. "At first he insisted on coming himself and bringing you directly home. You cannot imagine how difficult it was for me to convince him otherwise. Oh, Em, why did you have to *elope?*"

"I have not eloped, Sue. I have come to Springfield for a week's holiday."

"You don't even know these people—the Murrays."

"They are trusted friends of Judge Lord."

"But if you wanted to come to Springfield, surely you should have written Mary Holland or Elizabeth Bowles. Either would have been pleased to have you. And surely you should have confided in *me.*"

"I did as I thought best."

For the first few moments Emily had been so shocked and concerned at Sue's appearance that she could do no more than reply to Sue's barrage of questions and assault of insinuations. But then she gained control of her senses, and her immediate reaction was anger.

"I am not a child!" she snapped, "nor an animal to be led on a leash and obey a master's command!"

"You are a woman, Em—"

"A fact I have only recently rediscovered!"

"And Austin's sister. I cannot, in truth, champion Austin, but in this instance he holds the best motives."

"Unfortunately coupled with an obliquity of justice!" Emily paced up and down the length of the room. Her face was flushed and the veins in her throat taut, and she thought she might explode. "I am long past compromise, Sue. Even Austin must accept that. And he certainly knows Otis Lord is a respected and honorable man. A friend of our father's. One of Massachusetts' great men." She turned to face Sue. "And a widower. Remember that, Sue—a *widower.*"

"Em, Em—whom are you challenging? You know I am a romantic, and if you love the judge—"

"I do!" She caught her breath and wrapped her arms around herself as though racked with sudden pain. "Time has so escaped me, Sue, and I cannot drag it back from its silent grave. In Amherst, I listened to all the voices that gathered about me. In Amherst, I was and am possessed, haunted—like our house seems to be. Shall my darling Salem visit me there, where Mother lies a living corpse and Father's spirit is like a suffocating gray fog that seals you in a tunnel? Where I am mad, crazed, odd, *old maid* Emily Dickinson? No, no, *no!* No, Sue, no!"

Emily flung herself onto the sofa and turned her body away from Sue. Her shoulders heaved as she fought for breath, but she was not crying and her head never bowed.

Sue came instantly to her side and knelt down on the rug beside her. "Emily, dear. Please don't upset yourself so. I told you, I won this battle with Austin; if only all the others had also been fought and won." She sighed, and placed her arm across Emily's shoulders to reassure her. "I had to promise Austin that I would leave this house with you and take you with me to Mary Holland's, where I will be staying. But God forgive me, Em, if you wish, I shall break my word and leave you here. Though I don't know what I shall tell Mary." She removed her arm and clasped her hands in her lap as she sat back on her heels, looking much like a woman in prayer. "Or Austin either," she said softly and to herself.

Emily looked deeply into Sue's eyes. "I am sorry, Sue. Believe me, I am sorry. Perhaps I should not have been so secretive, but there seemed no other way. We plan to marry, Sue. Very soon."

"Oh, Em." Sue reached out her hand to Emily, and the two women clasped hands.

"I know Austin will never approve, but I have come to understand much about my brother that I did not before. He would approve no man who petitioned for my hand. He means me no injustice but he cannot see the truth or reality. He sees only his own image, and that is gathered in the gray ghost of our father. He would have approved no man either. And there is also Vinnie to contend with, for I have come to recognize the truth there, as well. If anyone is *queer* in our father's house, Sue, it is Vinnie. Vinnie, who believes she is still twenty. Vinnie, who believes Jack will come and take her with him one day. Vinnie, who is terrified that when that occurs, if I am not there to care for Mother, she will not be able to leave." Emily looked across the room. *"Summers of bloom, and months of frost, and days of jingling bells. Yet, all the while this hand upon our fireside . . ."*

She rose and stood by the flaming hearth. "I plan to watch Judge Lord preside over a murder case that begins tomorrow and I do not want you to come to the court-house with me." She turned. "If you were with me, my identity would easily be discovered. But that is not wholly the reason."

"It is your life, Em. Your experience. I understand."

"Yes—yes! My own!"

Beyond the closed door of the library new activity was taking place. The front door had opened and closed and children's gay voices could be heard in joyous greeting. Henry Murray had come home.

"I think I must meet my host," Emily said.

The two women faced each other and smiled nervously.

"You really plan to marry Otis Lord?" Sue asked.

"I do."

"Oh, how exciting it all is!" Sue laughed.

And when they opened the doors and were presented to Henry Murray, they looked like summers' past had just lighted up their eyes.

## 14

$\mathcal{T}$hough her father's profession was the law, Emily had never before entered a courtroom, either in or out of session. Edward Dickinson never permitted any of the Dickinson women to venture into the "real" world, and nowhere is reality so stark as in a courtroom.

Today Chloe Murray accompanied her to Judge Lord's court. There was a murmur as they took seats at the rear. Emily still wore her black veil and widow's dress, and for a brief moment the spectators, perhaps, thought she might be related to the defendants. A whisper passed from one to the other and heads turned surreptitiously. *Who was this mysterious woman in black?*

The courtroom was filled to overflowing. The space within the bar had been given up to women, and young children poked their curious faces between the railings of the gallery. Chloe leaned over to whisper to Emily that many of the "first families" of Springfield were represented, but Emily had already noted the crowd of well-dressed spectators and was not surprised, for she knew that the Kidder case was the most shocking crime to have been committed in Springfield in their time. It was not a simple case of violence among the immigrant and itinerant workers who were employed in the local factories. The Kidder family was upper-middle-class and fairly substantial. The father, Albert Kidder, had been a hard-working leather dealer who supplied holsters and belts to Smith and Wesson until his infirmity forced him to retire; his interest had been sold directly to that company when his sons refused to carry on for him.

*The Kidder twins*—bitter discussions about them raged in drawing rooms and offices of the city. It seemed far more heinous that one of "their own" had murdered his father in a fit of anger than had such a crime been committed among the "others." More especially since the two young men seemed to represent the alarming growth of free-licensed passions among well-educated, respectable middle-class sons. And to further increase the furor, one brother had stood with the other against the law, therefore condoning his twin's depravity. This also was a severe blow to Springfield's sense of probity.

Two chairs had been placed side by side in the dock for the defendants. The men had turned to face each other, and close, in that position, they looked a mirror image. As Emily studied them, even at her great distance, she believed she could never have been confused as to their individual identity. True, they were strikingly alike, *yet*—one seemed paler than the other, his hand trembled as he raised it to shade his eyes, as though the lights in the room were painful, and his body slumped; the other appeared as much at home as if he were at a gentlemen's club.

They shared dark good looks and lithe young bodies (they were twenty-four years of age), but the *pale one*, as Emily labeled him (for she did not yet know which was Dwight and which was Charles), was dressed in a casual, almost non-caring way, while the other appeared, though reasonably restrained, a dandy. No, she would not have had a problem identifying either of them. But then, she had not first seen them singly, as the witness had, nor in a moment of extreme agitation.

The case was considered so important that Attorney General Waterman was prosecuting for the Government against the Kidders. He was a very imposing gentleman (no one could call him otherwise, for he carried dignity and authority in his every gesture), a giant of a man, oversized in both height and breadth, and boldly sporting a large walrus mustache beneath a bulbous nose. He wore a pair of pince-nez glasses that gave the appearance of a mosquito stinging an elephant's trunk. Everywhere he moved, several assistants followed.

Mr. Leonard, the attorney for the defense, was a lean, dry man, dressed conservatively and much in the squire's style. In fact, he reminded Emily a good deal of her father. He sat at the defense table reading a document and making notes, conspicuously aloof in that crowded room, as though he had little connection with his clients and with the drama in which he was soon to play a leading role.

Crowded into the front section were seventy-four men and a single woman who had been summoned to potential jury duty.

"This morning they will select a jury," Chloe leaned over and whispered to Emily. "It might take up the entire day. Session closes at six, with a two-hour recess for lunch," she added.

Emily acknowledged the information with a sedate nod of her head.

"Oh, look over there—third row," Chloe said, her voice still hushed but the excitement growing in it. "Molly Parker! And there . . . last seats. Let's see, one, two . . . eighth row. The Dales! *Everyone's here.*" But Emily's attention was elsewhere, so Chloe settled back to search out Springfield's society for herself.

Never before had Emily been face to face with a killer. The thought that one man could kill another in cold blood was appalling to her. She had never been able to erase the wartime images from her mind. The devastation of the Civil War had not reached Amherst, nor echoes of the gunfire, but the village had not been spared. Very early in the war coffins had been sent home, and the roll call of those young men whom she had known since childhood began. Most vividly she remembered Frazer Stearns, killed in his very first battle. A hero's death, the report had been—for nineteen-year-old Frazer had single-handedly shot dead seven of the enemy who had infiltrated Union lines. Seven men shot dead by a boy who used to help her father with the horses and who had wept when one broke its leg and had to be destroyed.

Emily remembered Boston again and the curious journey she had taken to the grave of Dr. Webster, a condemned murderer, and how she had stood there feeling his presence at her feet, making her blood rush to her head and her breath chill within her. *How he must have suffered!* she had thought. And he *the guilty one.* However shocking her father might think such a reaction to be, she possessed the most consuming compassion for Dr. Webster, even knowing that pity for an educated man who had killed another doctor in his own laboratory was a blasphemous emotion. That dismal day, so filled with gray and mist and hauntings of her own, she had whispered words of forgiveness over Dr. Webster's grave. And she had been convinced, furthermore, that he had heard her speak, and that her words had eased his tortured soul.

But these young men—how could she feel compassion for either, knowing one had struck down his own father? Yet she did, overwhelmingly, and in fact, could feel the pain of compassion gripping her chest. *Oh, how they must be suffering! Oh, what agonies they must yet endure!*

"Hear ye! Hear ye! The case of the Commonwealth of Massachusetts against Dwight and Charles Kidder is now in session in this, the Supreme Court of Hampden County, Springfield, Massachusetts, on this day, the twenty-fifth of April, 1882, and presided over by his Honor, Judge Otis Lord. All rise."

Chloe had to press Emily's shoulder to convey to her that she must rise with the rest of the courtroom. Being so small and at the rear, she was unable to see the judge enter his "court." She imagined he did so with a kingly presence and felt intense pride at that thought.

"You may be seated," the usher said.

Emily remained standing.

"Emily . . ." Chloe warned in a whisper.

Emily obeyed, but in a state of shock. Her Salem, the kindly mentor, *lover*, wore black robes and sat stiffly, his eyes unsmiling, glancing out over his courtroom not as a king who must have mercy for his subjects, but as a judge who must scourge them for the truth and sentence them for their crimes. Emily was shaken, terrified.

*Have you ever sentenced a man to die?* she had asked him once.

*Yes* had been his reply.

Her black dress now seemed most fitting. What else could one wear to a place where men were on trial for their lives? What else should one wear in a room where the human spirit must die more than once before sentence? She understood now why a judge wore black robes.

"It's shocking. They are so young! And that one—the one on the *left*—most attractive!" Chloe whispered.

"To murder one's father." She shuddered. "Dreadful!"

Emily just nodded and sat forward on the edge of the hard wood bench, watching attentively every moment through the long hours of the morning, but at the back of her mind she was storing up questions:

*What do you feel up there?*
*Are you filled with your own sense of power?*
*Are you overcome with compassion?*
*Are you the man I know?*
*Are you still my darling Salem?*

One by one the potential jurors crossed to the witness stand, took the oath, and answered the many questions. Emily was hypnotized by it all. The two men she truly loved in her life—her father and Otis—were practitioners of the law. Yet, this was the first time she had ever seen the machinery of their trade and realized how it could affect them. She understood now her father's lack of humor, his impatience with emotion, his authoritative and ofttimes frightening manner. He had been shaped and hardened in similar courtrooms. Yet with Otis, it seemed to have worked in reverse. He always seemed to have a ready smile and did not turn away from emotions, not even his own.

She studied the Kidder twins. *But they must fear Otis,* she thought. The idea shocked her. *And Mr. Leonard, and Mr. Waterman as well, and all those prospective jurors who each in his or her turn glanced nervously in his direction—they must fear Otis.* Her mouth felt dry. And at this moment she felt her heart turn over. *I fear Otis,* she thought with surprise.

She remained in a shocked state until the court recessed for lunch. The two women returned to the Murray house. For Emily the time would seem endless until she could return to that courtroom. Somehow, whatever judgment waited there belonged in small measure to her as well as to the young men on trial.

*15*

Talk at the luncheon table centered on the one woman who had been selected to serve on the jury, but Emily contributed very little. Her mind was focused somewhere along the path of midday sun that flooded the room, her anguish there for the discerning to see. Miss DePeters caught the turmoil in one glance, and then, fearing her discovery might seem threatening to Emily, looked immediately away.

This gesture did not escape Emily, for at that moment she had been looking, almost unseeing, at Shauna DePeters, erect in the rosewood chair, so smartly dressed in a high-necked, slim-waisted polished calico the color of ripe wheat, yet so exotic with her thick black hair coiled in braids around the smooth crown of her head.

After lunch Emily went directly to her room; she had a great need to be alone for a while before the hansom came to carry them back to the courthouse for the afternoon's session.

She stood at the porthole window and the room became a ship's cabin, the lawns a smooth sea. She was, she felt, setting out on a journey, and all the courage and sense of adventure that had aided in bringing her to Springfield seemed now, as her boat began to lift anchor, to be slipping away.

She realized that for so many years had her life been contained within her father's boundaries, she now felt discomfited elsewhere, disoriented. The knowledge brought a terror to her soul. For how could she cope in a wifely role with a man as socially integrated as Otis? Could she expect him to create another refuge for her to commune with the muses? And was he, after all, not Otis, not Salem, but *the judge?*

The questions whirred in her head and made her dizzy, and she turned away from the window.

Could it possibly be that she had become so expert in the management of grief that she no longer could deal with joy? For years she had had no company other than her poetry. Was she now and forever a stranger to all else?

Years before—just after the war—she had written a poem for Sue:

> *Safe in their Alabaster Chambers—*
> *Untouched by Morning—*
> *And untouched by Noon-*
> *Lie the meek members of the Resurrection-*
> *Rafter of satin–and Roof of Stone!*

Had her father's house been her alabaster chamber, had the mortal Emily died, so that she could no longer be touched? She knew this was untrue. She had inherited a fortitude from her father that gave her the ability to endure, and she had, as well, an unquenchable joy in existence. She staunchly believed that she must seize what little time there was to live.

Her thirst for experience had led her to Springfield;

her love for Otis would bring her strength to refuse any compromise with destiny.

Returning to the window and looking across the great expanse of emerald grass and past the age-old trees to catch a glimpse of the city's life, she thought: *How many hours have I spent before my own window studying the pageant of Main Street?* She had attentively studied the passing figures, for sooner or later all the inhabitants of Amherst had passed by her father's house. She had noted intently their gait and gesture, and learned to judge from these whether the person had any meat within, whether there was any anthracite in their veins. Otis did. She could not allow anything so small as this present discomfort to keep them apart. She could not spend the rest of her years looking at life from a third-floor window where the perspective raised her above and beyond it.

There was a gentle knock at her door though she had heard no one approach. For a moment she wavered, unsure if she should answer. Then, crossing to the door, she unlocked it, and with a touch of bravado, opened it wide.

Shauna DePeters looked at her, unblinking. "The hansom is waiting," she announced.

"Thank you."

Miss DePeters turned to go.

"Miss DePeters—" The girl faced Emily but she was partially concealed by the shadow. Emily stepped out of her room and into the hallway. "Would you be kind enough to tell Mrs. Murray I will be right down?" she asked.

The young woman nodded her head and for a brief moment her eyes betrayed her and Emily was able to see *in.* Pain reposed uneasily there, apparently a long-time resident. Well, pain that was worthy did not go soon.

"I am sorry," Miss DePeters said before she descended the stairs.

Emily understood that Miss DePeters knew she had revealed herself in that momentary flash and that the Indian girl considered her own openness a breach of etiquette.

"Miss DePeters," Emily called after her.

The lean figure poised in flight, and Emily, as though approaching a bird in her garden, took several cautious steps toward her.

"I like a look of agony," Emily said softly, "because I know it is true."

There was a static moment between the two women, but it was Emily who turned away first and disappeared through the shadows to fetch her cloak.

> *For each ecstatic instant*
> *We must an anguish pay*
> *In keen and quivering ratio*
> *To the ecstasy.*

*P*erhaps what the judge most
respected was justice, and what pained him most was
injustice. When as a young man he had first come to
Springfield, the old courthouse was still in use, and one
of his daily duties as a law clerk was to carry briefs from
his office there. Outside that plain wooden building,
which for many years had been the only public building
in town, stood the old whipping post. He had never
overcome his agony at the sight of it, and had only been
pleased to return to Springfield when the new courthouse had been erected and the whipping post destroyed.

He knew his interpretation of justice and injustice
was not always the same as his colleagues', and this was
a constant source of unhappiness to him. They considered him to be a reformer and even radical. His views
had not made him popular with his peers, but they had
with the galleries and the press. He was a conscionable
man and was never able to forget that society sat in the
dock along with every man or woman on trial. It seemed
to him, in fact, that he never had the blessed faculty of

forgetting that responsibility as some men did.

There was, for example, the glass case in the foyer of the present courthouse. Displayed inside it were old handcuffs, ankle chains, and the most horrifying item of all—a leather collar worn by a man in bond during the seventeenth century. A piece of strong leather, about two fingers wide, its ends were riveted together with nails of copper, so that it could not be removed except by a blacksmith. On a ring in front was a brass tally with the initials of the poor wretch's master carved into it. Judge Lord's heart heaved over with the thought of a man having to wear such a symbol of man's inhumanity. How capable man was of wounding another man's spirit! Did not the *master* bear his portion of guilt? Must he not be made to pay for the arrogance that would allow him to carve his initials into another man's bond?

The judge sighed. He was very aware that men's lives were in his hands, and he did not bear the responsibility easily. If both or either of the Kidders was found guilty, he would necessarily have to condemn them to death or to a long prison term. Of these options, he ofttimes thought the former, considering the faulty penal system, preferable. If sentenced to prison on such grave charges, it would mean these young men would go to jail as youths and come out as middle-aged or old men —if they came out at all. What chance would such men have for reform or usefulness after an incarceration filled with horror and indignity and exposure to the worst elements in life? Hardly any at all, and the State scarcely pretended otherwise. It simply said that society was no longer safe if such men were allowed to remain at large, and the men themselves were cast like rubbish in the void.

Such considerations might indicate that the judge

was more fitted for philanthropy than for the bench, or that his verdicts might be light-handed. Neither was the case. Otis Lord was a man dedicated to justice and reared in the law. He earnestly believed that the only way to overcome injustice was by changing society, but he still could see no other alternative than to do so *through* the law. He could, therefore, in good though pained conscience, condemn a guilty man to prison or death, and at the same time work for and be outspoken in support of prison reform.

There was no doubt in his mind that upon the unfolding of all the facts in the Kidder case, justice would prevail. He doubted neither his own conscience nor the moral turpitude of his colleagues. Pressure had already been exerted upon him by the political and clerical leaders of the county. Most naturally, such pressure had been in the most correct and circumspect manner, but the style merely screened the lobbying he was subject to.

The rise of promiscuity in alcohol, sex, and violence among the youth of the state, together with the availability of handguns, was an abrasive statistical reality to the present administration, and the press had made it an issue of condemnation. If he had not been his own man, the judge could easily have been smashed by the vise both parties placed him in. It was because of such deviltry and unfriendly persuasion that he was convinced his refusal to be a political candidate on any ticket was valid. His first allegiance was and must remain with justice and the law.

But the judge now set all these thoughts aside as he sat in chambers between sessions. The usher shook his head knowingly as he passed the half-opened door, saying to himself that it was the gravity of judicial responsibility that caused the judge to sit there so owl-like, seeming so shatteringly alone. Had he known how distant the judge's mind was he would have been disappointed; for he was a man who was very proud of his perceptions.

The judge pulled at his shaggy eyebrows as it occurred to him that the events of the week might become too difficult for Emily to bear. He might, in bringing her to Springfield and exposing her to such environmental differences, subject her to an adverse reaction. She might —she *could*—withdraw, return to Amherst, and chaining the door, remove herself forever from the possibility of a life with him.

Emily was not like other women. He knew she would never be happy with the same frivolities most of them might use to occupy their time or thoughts. And with her overwhelming emotions and sensitivities, he could not predict how she might respond to the unusual circumstances of the Kidder trial.

The usher tapped discreetly at the door and peered in. "Your Honor," he said as he cleared his throat and then glanced at the wall clock to indicate his mission.

"Yes, yes. Thank you," the judge replied. He waited until the man was gone before rising. Then, with a slow step, he left his chambers and walked down the center hallway of the courthouse to the staircase that ascended to the courtroom on the floor above. He had memorized all the portraits hung on the walls. There was no need to look at them. And he chose not to acknowledge clerks or colleagues either upon entering or departing a courtroom.

He used the private passageway to the courtroom provided for judges and members of the bar. Then, like an actor waiting for his cue, he stood for a brief moment in the anteroom.

"Hear ye, hear ye—"
Otis Lord glanced up at the ceiling. It was ash wood,

as was the ceiling and the walls of the room beyond. The motif disturbed him and the wood gave off a dry, aging scent. And so it was difficult for the judge to cast off a feeling of entombment as he entered his court.

All heads in the courtroom were bowed as the clergyman intoned the prayer:

"Blessed is the man that walketh not in the counsel of the ungodly. Nor standeth in the way of sinners, nor sitteth in the seat of the scornful.

"But his delight is in the law of the LORD; and in his law doth he meditate day and night.

"And he shall be like a tree planted by the rivers of water that bringeth forth its fruit in his season; his leaf also shall not wither; and whatsoever he doeth shall prosper.

"The ungodly *are* not so; but *are* like the chaff which the wind driveth away.

"Therefore the ungodly shall not stand in the judgement, nor sinners in the congregation of the righteous.

"For the LORD knoweth the way of the righteous, but the way of the ungodly shall perish. Amen."

There was a taut silence in the courtroom, as though all present were holding it grasped tightly to them. The jury had duly been selected and the trial was about to begin. The members of the jury sat forward in their seats. Something in their expressions gave them the look of people of a special solemnity. Short hours before, they had been average citizens: farmers, shopkeepers; the woman, Eliza Goodlift, was a milliner. But as members of the jury, they looked from the defendants to the counsels to the spectators with an air of aloofness, as though their new status made the rest of the court, exclusive of the judge, inferior to them. The foreman, Ebenezer Thrasher, cast a decidedly malevolent side glance at the Goodlift woman, who, in deference, had been placed beside him. She leaned back and folded her hands in her lap, interlocking her long delicate fingers to keep them still. She was nervous, but not without control.

"Proceed with the reading of the indictment," Judge Lord ordered.

"The people of the Commonwealth of Massachusetts charge that Dwight Kidder of 13 Carew Street, Springfield, in the County of Hampden, and Charles Kidder, a registered voter of that same address, did feloniously, willfully, and with malice aforethought conspire to murder and then did make an assault on and shoot dead their father, Albert Kidder, on the seventh night of June in the year of our Lord one thousand and eight hundred and eighty-one, at his home and his place of residence, 13 Carew Street, Springfield, in the County of Hampden. The case is now declared opened."

Attorney General Waterman rose to his feet. "Your Honor."

"Do you have an opening statement to present to the court, Mr. Waterman?"

"I do, indeed."

"Proceed."

Judge Lord sat poised, waiting. One hand rested upon his gavel, the other held a pencil which he pressed, as though it supported his arm, on an unmarked pad. Presumably, pad and pencil were for him to make notes. Instead, his habit was to use the paper for sketching when the courtroom proceedings grew tedious. He was a fair caricaturist, and few who were involved in cases before him were spared the revelation of his drawings, for though he considered himself an intensely just man, his pencil work was rapier-sharp and often prejudicial.

"Where, *where*," the attorney general was saying as he faced the jury, "where have you heard or known of so heinous a crime being committed? Two brothers, twins, with but one evil thought, a single-mindedness of such a deep dye as to seem Mephistophelian. *Patricide.* To utter the word renders one faint. And, gentlemen— rather, *lady* and gentlemen—of the jury, I am trusting you are not of faint heart, for in the testimony to follow you will be witness to words spoken on oath that shall, the state persists, prove beyond any question of doubt that these two men you see in the dock have been so steeped in vice, so sunk in iniquity, so bereft of morality, to render them capable of such a horror as . . . *patricide.*"

He turned away and his vast body quivered in anquish. Then he sighed deeply, drew himself up to his full and imposing height, and with a quick step crossed to his table, distractedly sorting through some papers, a pained scowl furrowing his forehead.

"Your Honor, I would like to call Chief Medical Examiner Arthur Brock to the stand as the prosecution's first witness," he said.

"Unless procedure has changed since I was last on the bench, Mr. Waterman, I believe the defense also has the right to address the jury and the court."

"My apologies, your Honor, to both you and my colleague. I fear the terrible gravity of this case has seized me."

Mr. Leonard, counsel for the defense, rose slowly to his feet. His face gave no indication of either turmoil or insult or anger, as if his opponent's accusations were beneath his reaction.

"I am in hopes the court will not be confused, your Honor, for it did sound as if Mr. Waterman was entering a closing not an opening argument into the record. I would, if I may, simply like to reassure one and all that, indeed, the case has just been opened. At the same time I should like to acknowledge that I know all present to be of fair, moral, and civilized persuasion, incapable of such prejudicial prejudgment as Mr. Waterman would seem to encourage. I am here to prove my clients innocent of the charges the Commonwealth of Massachusetts has brought against them and to fight for each citizen's undeniable right under our state constitution of a fair trial based on the facts in the case and not upon the fears and guilts of society. I would be pleased, your Honor, to listen attentively if Mr. Waterman now cares to call his first witness."

"Mr. Arthur Brock to the stand, please."

As chief medical examiner, this was not Arthur Brock's first court appearance. He strode to the stand with great assurance.

"Your hand on the Book, please. Do you swear to tell the truth, the whole truth, and nothing but the truth, so help you God?"

"I do."

"Proceed."

Mr. Waterman stood behind the prosecution's table, narrowing his eyes as he held his pince-nez glasses in his hand. His voice was loud and authoritative and no one in the courtroom had any difficulty at all hearing his every word.

"Now, Mr. Brock, on the night of the seventh of June last year, the court understands that you were called to the residence of the deceased, Mr. Albert Kidder, in the persuance of your profession. Would you be kind enough to tell the court the circumstances."

"I was called by Dr. Nathanial Crane after he had pronounced Mr. Albert Kidder dead."

"Did Dr. Crane come personally to fetch you?"

"He did, and I walked with him to 13 Carew Street."

"I see. And when you arrived, was anyone else present in the Kidder residence?"

"The servant girl. She was sitting in the kitchen and

was quite distraught. Dr. Crane showed me where the corpse was and returned to administer to the girl."

"What were your findings upon examining the corpse, Mr. Brock?"

"Well, of course, they could only be cursory and not conclusive. The following morning the corpse was examined in proper conditions and an autopsy performed, but that night it appeared that the deceased had died of gunshot wounds and that they could not have been self-inflicted." Here, Arthur Brock paused, as if there was something further on his mind.

"Is something troubling you, Mr. Brock?"

"The deceased also had a very nasty bruise on the side of his head," the man said slowly.

"Did you conclude this was caused by his fall?"

"I am a professional man, sir, and I conclude nothing until proper medical proof is available."

"Mr. Brock, did this 'nasty bruise' raise any questions in your mind?"

"It was not on the side of his head that would have struck the ground in the fall that placed his body as I found it."

"Would you say, Mr. Brock, that the bruise indicated something of greater violence than a fall?"

"As I said, sir, I never presume or set forth indications. The bruise was, however, exceedingly nasty, and the deceased, for I had known him, had been elderly and infirm. I was, therefore, distressed that he had suffered such a grievous blow, though I could not ascertain at that moment the weapon used, but the autopsy disclosed that it was caused by the butt of a gun swung at considerable force and at very close range."

"And would you tell the court the remainder of the autopsy's findings?"

"There was a wound on the left arm, three and one

half inches below the shoulder joint, and the autopsy revealed the fact that the ball had passed through the arm and entered the body between the fourth and fifth ribs, shattering the latter and piercing the aorta, thereby immediately emptying the heart of blood. From the appearance of the wound, Mr. Kidder must have been positioned sideways from the person who fired the shot. The wound was necessarily fatal in a moment or two after it was received." Arthur Brock paused, and then recalling something else, continued. "Oh, yes, the course of the ball was a trifle downward."

"What does that imply, Mr. Brock?"

"That the ball had been shot by a man or woman no more than a few inches above Mr. Kidder."

"The court appreciates your thoroughness, Mr. Brock. Now could you return to 13 Carew Street that night and tell the court of any further observations you made while there?"

"There was a painting hanging over Mr. Kidder's bed that I momentarily thought to be a likeness of either Dwight or Charles Kidder, until I realized the painting was of a young man dressed as young men did, oh, somewhere in the thirties, I would say. It was, of course, a portrait of Mr. Kidder, but I was struck for the first time with how very much his sons resembled him. It was the first chance I had had to think of those the poor man had left behind."

"And what were your thoughts, sir?"

"Filled with sorrow. How could they be other when one contemplated such an ill and elderly man being struck down so? It never passed my mind at the time that such a crime could have been perpetrated by a member of the dead man's own family."

"Objection!"

"Strike Mr. Brock's last words from the record,"

Judge Lord ordered immediately. "May I remind you, Mr. Brock," he admonished the witness, "that it has not been proved yet who was responsible for Mr. Kidder's murder?"

Mr. Waterman had turned, and as though anticipating his wishes, an assistant instantly stepped forward with a jar. The attorney general walked to the witness stand and handed the specimen to Brock.

"What does this jar contain, Mr. Brock?" he inquired.

"The section of the aorta damaged in the fatal shot, and belonging to Mr. Kidder."

"You are quite certain of this?"

"Most certainly! I placed it in this container myself and labeled it by my own hand."

"I would like to present this jar and its contents as evidence for the jury's inspection, your Honor."

"Agreed."

The assistant stepped up again, and taking the evidence, crossed with it to the jury. Everyone turned to look at the lone woman juror. Eliza Goodlift was the first to take the glass bottle in her hands.

"Thank you, Mr. Brock," Mr. Waterman said.

"Is that all?"

"Unless there is something you have neglected to tell the court."

"There is not."

"Your witness, Mr. Leonard."

"No questions."

"Dismissed."

Arthur Brock rose rather ceremoniously and walked directly up the center aisle. As he passed Emily, Brock glanced over at her, her mourning dress attracting his notice.

The man's glance was as cold as steel, as cutting as

a scalpel, and Emily was relieved when he passed her by and left the courtroom. That same glance had probed the dead, was intimate with death. Emily, since her father's passing, believed herself to be intimate with death, but she had never thought of the dead as inanimate flesh that could be explored. No, to her death meant that the flesh had surrendered, and left only the soul. Death was a dialogue between spirit and flesh, in which spirit prevailed. Believing this, she could accept and make peace with death, and so, the mental image the medical examiner brought to her was excruciatingly painful.

"Would you care to leave?" Chloe whispered.

"No." Emily straightened on the hard bench and concentrated her attention on the two men in the dock. They sat side by side, with enough distance between them so that the observer could frame each as though he were alone. But for Emily, the two faces continually merged into one, and that one not quite either of them. They were the face of their father in the portrait of him as a young man—the one Arthur Brock had mentioned. At the same time they were the daguerreotype of her own father that sat on the table beside her mother's bed.

How could it be possible to snuff out the life of one's own parent? To contemplate the terrible passions that could motivate such a crime almost overwhelmed Emily. She had to grip the hardwood armrests with all her might to keep from slipping to the floor, and she sat quite still until the wave of faintness passed.

# 17

The Kidder twins were once again two faces. A young woman was taking the stand. Judge Lord leaned forward, studying the girl.

"Do you swear to tell the truth, the whole truth, and nothing but the truth, so help you God?"

Softly, "I do."

"Your name, please?"

"Maud"—she paused to clear her throat—"Maud Hagarty."

"Are you a spinster or a married woman?"

"I am—unmarried, sir."

"Where do you reside?"

"Thirteen Carew Street."

Her words were almost inaudible. Judge Lord looked down at her and said, "You will have to speak up, young woman. There is nothing to fear."

She nodded her head and took a deep breath. Mr. Waterman rose and advanced toward her, and for an instant she cowered in her chair, but then she drew herself up and squared her shoulders, and though she looked very much like a woman in pain, she did not tremble or avoid Mr. Waterman's eyes.

"How old are you, Miss Hagarty?" he asked.

"Three and twenty, sir."

"And what is your occupation?"

"I am a servant girl, sir."

"Were you employed as such on the night of June seventh last?"

"Yes, sir."

"Where and for whom?"

"For Mr. Albert Kidder, sir, at 13 Carew Street."

"You still reside at that address?"

"Yes, sir. The young Mr. Kidders asked me to stay on. I be working for their father, sir, since I was fifteen. I knew no other home."

For a brief moment her composure seemed in danger of collapsing, but Mr. Waterman caught this and stepped in closer. He spoke to her in a kindly paternal tone. "Miss Hagarty, the court understands that you have undergone a grievous ordeal, but could you bear to relate to us the sequence of events from your own point of view on that terrible night of June seventh last?"

"I . . . I will try, sir." She cleared her throat and glanced nervously at the two men in the dock before she continued. "It was Sunday and me day off. I was not to be home until six and was not required to prepare supper. But, as I said, sir, I knew no other home. I had visited the graves of me parents in the afternoon and returned about half past five. I was surprised to discover that Mr. Charles had come home."

"Why is that so? Was it not his home as well?"

"His room was always waiting, sir, if that be what you mean, but he traveled about a good deal."

"How much time would you consider to be a good deal, Miss Hagarty?"

"He had not been to home in over a year, sir. February fifteenth it had been, and just after St. Valentine's Day. He brought me a length of English cloth to make a frock for church. I shall never be forgetting."

"Were you especially fond of Mr. Charles?"

She stiffened. "All three of the Misters had been kind to me."

"But were you fonder of Mr. Charles than of his brother or his father?"

"No, sir, but as he was away so often and had so many stories to tell when he did return, and because Mr. Charles has the gift for speech, sir, I always enjoyed his homecomings."

"I see."

"I sincerely hope you do, sir," she said primly. "I be just a servant girl, sir, orphaned and plain. The clerk asked if I be spinster, and I said unmarried, but I have had no offers from young men and guess I be that, after all, sir, and shall remain one. Mr. Charles, well . . . you can see that clearly we are not of . . . the same cloth, sir. Mr. Charles would never . . . Well, you understand, sir." Her voice grew very soft and she appeared flushed, and she kept her eyes lowered as though she were studying her worn, ringless hands.

"And on your part, Miss Hagarty, did you ever dare to hope he might come to regard you as a young woman and not as Maud Hagarty the servant girl?"

The girl drew quickly to attention. Her face turned crimson and there was anger in her eyes. "Certainly not, sir! I know me station!"

"Yes, of course." He turned away and drew closer to the jury. "Now, Miss Hagarty, would you be kind enough to continue with the events of June seventh last?"

"Well, I did not see Mr. Charles. I always enter from the rear, and I went straightaways to the kitchen. The kettle was up and Mr. Dwight had prepared a tray, as he often did on me off days, for hisself and for Mr. Kidder. But that night there be three plates of cold meat—I had prepared a roast the night before—and three cups waiting to be filled with tea."

"Could there not have been another guest in the house?"

"Maybe, sir, but I knew it to be Mr. Charles. On the kitchen table was a package with me name on it." She smiled tentatively. "A lovely feather plume, sir, the likes of which I had never seen close up."

"And was there a note with this gift?"

"No, sir, but no one else but Mr. Charles would have brung me such a present, and me name was inscribed in his very own hand."

"Continue the sequence of events, Miss Hagarty."

"Well, when I saw Mr. Charles must be home, I thought it would be more a homecoming if I fixed something hot with their supper, so I went to fetch some beans to warm. They be stored in the larder, just outside the kitchen. It was then that I heared voices . . ."

"What kind of voices did you hear?"

"Theirs, of course. Well, I could not be sure of that. But men's voices, very loud, coming from Mr. Kidder's room, which be above the kitchen, with the window just over the larder."

"Could you hear what they said?"

"No, sir. The window was closed. Mr. Kidder was very ill, sir. We never left him in a draft. Anyway, I did not stop to listen. I went back into the kitchen with the beans."

"Was it not unusual to hear an argument emanating from the room of an infirm and elderly man?"

Maud Hagarty allowed a nervous look over to the dock, then she drew it quickly away. "Well, somewhat, sir."

"*Somewhat* unusual, Miss Hagarty? What does that mean to imply?"

Once more her gaze darted to the dock and back again. "Must I reply, sir?"

"I remind you, Miss Hagarty, that you have sworn an oath on the Holy Bible."

Very softly, "Mr. Charles and Mr. Kidder did not see eye to eye, sir."

"They argued whenever he did come home then, is that correct?"

Softer still, "Yes . . . sir . . ."

"In fact, would you say that these arguments Charles Kidder had with his father were responsible for his absences from his home and the reason for his lack of contributing to the care of this unfortunate and elderly old man?"

"I object, your Honor," Mr. Leonard interrupted. "Mr. Waterman is asking the witness a question she can only answer with supposition."

"The court quite agrees, Mr. Leonard. Strike the question from the record."

"Thank you, your Honor." Mr. Leonard sat down.

"Had anyone confided to you the reason for the arguments that took place whenever Mr. Charles came home?" the prosecutor continued.

"Mr. Charles was deeply concerned about Mr. Dwight, sir. They be very close, being twins and all, and growing up in a motherless home. Mr. Charles would tell me I should make Mr. Dwight leave the house more, things like that. And that Mr. Kidder was robbing Mr. Dwight of the only treasure any of us had—our youth."

"Do you believe youth is our only treasure, Miss Hagarty?"

"No, sir. Belief in the Almighty is me greatest treasure."

"And exactly right! Now continue, Miss Hagarty."

"Let me see . . . Well, I went back to the kitchen and I heared this terrible scuffling over me head."

"Did you hear anything else?"

"Shouts, terrible screams . . . and then . . . yes, then gunshots. And then a sound like someone had fallen to the floor. And then more shots. No—*one* more shot only."

"What did you do?"

"I . . . I . . . run out of the house to fetch Dr. Crane, as he lives only a short distance away."

"You did not go up to Mr. Kidder's room to investigate?"

"Oh, no, sir!"

"And no one came down to the kitchen?"

"It was only a moment or two, I am sure, before I run from the house."

"Were you frightened that if Mr. Charles or Mr. Dwight found you in the kitchen your life might be in danger?"

"Objection, your Honor. It has not been proved that, in fact, Dwight or Charles Kidder *was* present in the house, or that it was either or both of them whom the witness heard."

"Sustained."

"Were you frightened that *whoever* was in the house might find you and might do you personal harm?"

"No, sir, not that. I never give it any other thought but that it be Mr. Charles and Mr. Dwight and Mr. Kidder. I was frightened because I knew something terrible had happened. I never thought that it be Mr. Kidder who . . . who . . . might have suffered so. I thought . . ." she stopped.

"Yes, Miss Hagarty?"

"I don't think that gentleman will permit me to say," she said pointing to Mr. Leonard.

"I am the judge of this court, Miss Hagarty," Judge Lord assured her. "If you will explain to us first why you came to think whatever it is you thought at the time, you may continue."

She paused, considering it, and then with a noticeable tremor in her voice, began. "Mr. Kidder had asked Mr. Charles many times to return home for good. He had cut off his allowance, but Mr. Charles didn't seem to mind. The one thing he truly seemed to mind was Mr. Dwight having to remain in the house."

She glanced over to the dock, her face flushed with nervousness. Then she quickly turned aside and cast her glance downward to study her red, worn hands. "Mr. Dwight told me that Mr. Charles wanted his father to go to hospital and so free Mr. Dwight of his duties, but Mr. Dwight never complained and Mr. Kidder would not hear of such a plan. But Mr. Charles was so . . . so . . . *certain* this be wrong. It made him very angry and he said terrible things to his father when he had last been to home."

"Would you say he threatened his father?"

"Oh, no, sir! But he was very angry, and Mr. Charles—" She looked up and bit her lip, as though angry at herself for what she had just said. It was a moment before she could go on. "Mr. Charles is a mite excitable," she said in an apologetic voice, "and there have always been so many guns around the house. There was one just beside Mr. Kidder's bed. Well, his being connected with Smith and Wesson and all that . . . I thought . . . I *feared* . . ."

"Yes, Miss Hagarty, the court is waiting patiently."

"That Mr. Kidder had shot Mr. Charles after Mr. Charles said something terrible." The words seemed to rush from her.

"But Mr. Kidder was unable to move from his bed,

Miss Hagarty. How did you explain that to yourself?"

"He had very strong arms, and he had been a guns-man all his life, sir."

"So you ran to fetch Dr. Crane, thinking Charles Kidder might be wounded. Is that correct?"

"Yes, sir."

"Tell the court what happened then, please."

"Dr. Crane came directly back with me. The house was silent and he told me to remain in the kitchen and he would go to investigate. He come downstairs a few moments later and into the kitchen and says, 'Mr. Kidder is dead, Maud.' "

"What did you reply?"

" 'Which Mr. Kidder, sir?' He told me then it be the old gentleman and that there was no one else in the house. He asked me to stay until he come back, and I sat in the kitchen all the time. It seemed terrible long, but I fancy it was no more than five or ten minutes. He returned with Mr. Brock. Then he give me something to take and asks me if I wanted to spend the night with his family, but I thanked him and went to me own room, which is behind the kitchen."

"Did anyone enter the house during the night?"

"No, sir."

"Weren't you expecting either Dwight or Charles Kidder to return?"

"I was, but they never come."

"They had both vanished into the air during the time you went to fetch Dr. Crane. Is that correct?"

"Well, they was gone when I returned."

"So you were in the house alone that night, except for the corpse of Albert Kidder?"

Maud Hagarty shivered. "Yes, sir. And I remained in me room until the next morning after they come and took Mr. Kidder away, not wanting to see such a sight, sir."

"Thank you, Miss Hagarty. Your witness, Mr. Leonard."

Judge Lord leaned down. "Are you feeling strong enough to continue, Miss Hagarty?" he inquired.

"I think so, your Honor."

"Proceed, Mr. Leonard."

"Miss Hagarty, I ask you to return to a point in time when you entered the Kidder house the night under discussion."

"Yes, sir."

"You saw no one, correct?"

"No one, sir."

"And you could not positively identify any of the voices coming from Mr. Kidder's room?"

"No, sir. They were unnatural due to the fighting, and muffled, as the window was closed."

"So in absolute truth, you had no way of knowing for certain who *other* than Mr. Kidder was in the house and in his room?"

"No, sir, but I supposed . . ."

"For *certain*, Miss Hagarty."

"No, sir, you are right. I was not certain."

"And you saw no one after the gunshots?"

"That be right, sir."

"And the house was empty of all save a corpse as far as you and Dr. Crane could ascertain when you returned with him?"

"Right, sir."

"Then, Miss Hagarty—and remember you have sworn on oath on the Holy Bible—are you able to tell this court now that you knew unequivocally, and disregarding such circumstantial evidence as supposition, that the defendants Charles and Dwight Kidder were in the house on Carew Street and in their father's room at the time you heard the fight and the gunshots?"

"I . . . I cannot, sir."

"That is all, Miss Hagarty. I thank you very much."

Maud Hagarty looked bewildered.

"You may step down," Judge Lord told her as he signaled the bailiff to help her from the stand.

They crossed the enclosure together, the bailiff holding her elbow. As she passed the Kidder brothers, her eyes filled with tears. Charles smiled at her and nodded his head. She went on past the enclosure and up the aisle and to the gallery, but her soft sobs could still be heard.

Emily fixed her gaze on the two men in the dock. They had been moved by the girl's testimony and by her show of emotion. Emily's heart turned. To Maud Hagarty these were not two men standing trial for murder, they were the only close ties she had in this world.

It was a fine, still morning, the earth bound in hard, mute, glittering frost, and Emily stood at her ship's-eye window, surveying the scene beyond. The vast old leafless maples and elms staunchly guarded the grounds, yet the day was not harsh. There was a light in spring that did not exist in other seasons, and it seemed to Emily that the light had form, perhaps a ghostly shape of past springs or of springs to come.

Her thoughts had been filled with ghosts since the end of the previous day's court session. And in the evening she had been so distraught, she had not been able to face Otis, even though she knew the anguish he must be suffering at her rejection. She had even refused to see Sue, who had come by to talk to her.

The image that haunted her most had not yet been described in the courtroom. It was the murder scene in Albert Kidder's bedroom. No one could detail those moments, of course, except the men who had been in that room. Still, as if she were present, she had been blinded by the brilliance of those gun explosions, had turned away from the old man's face in the agony of dying, and most painful, had been unable to pull her mind's eye away from the sight of that empty bed, the frail impression left upon the crumpled sheets.

Emily knew now what her father had spared her and what Austin wanted to spare her. They were both aware of how sensitive she was to the sorrow of others. They had seen her bend when the wind grew too strong, and fearing she would break, had protected her from storms outside. Had they done right? She wasn't sure, for now she seemed unable to cope with harsh reality. And if she was to be Mrs. Justice Lord, by God, she must!

By this early dawn hour, at home, she would have pumped the water and built and lighted the fires and begun baking bread. But she was a stranger in the Murray household, and its silence told her the others were not awake. Though the confinement of her room was becoming almost too difficult to bear, propriety caused her to hesitate before leaving it and venturing downstairs.

In the end, her distress won and she dressed hurriedly. Wrapping herself well in her shawl, she cautiously opened the door of her room, then made her way quietly down the corridor to the stairway. The large house was silent except for a floorboard that creaked with the cold and a shade flapping on an opened window on the landing below. Emily walked on tiptoe, holding her skirts to her so that they would not rustle. She took each step slowly, quietly, pausing and listening each time before continuing her descent. The sun was not yet high enough for the light to come through the stairwell windows, so she walked in grayness, moving in and out of darker and lighter patches, weaving a tapestry in black and gray. She stood in the downstairs reception hall at the bottom of the three flights of stairs, and waited for several moments.

The front door was bolted from the inside and opening it might cause too loud a noise. She decided instead to go into the kitchen and out the rear of the house. Turning carefully on her heel, she gently opened the door to the pantry and kitchen.

Miss DePeters, dressed and groomed for the day, sat at the table drinking tea; a fire freshly lit in the kitchen hearth filled the room with its warmth and sound. Miss DePeters rose instantly as Emily paused in the entrance.

"Shall I get you some tea, Miss Dickinson?" she asked in a voice as diffident and yet as pleasing as the sound of a soft breeze among leaves.

"No, thank you. And please return to yours."

"Agnes doesn't rise till half past six, and breakfast won't be served before eight." She said it apologetically, not meaning to intrude upon Emily's desires.

"I thought I might take a walk first. Have you been out?"

"I always get up with the first light and greet the day on my own."

"We have much in common, Miss DePeters."

"Are you feeling better this morning?"

"Last night—Oh, dear"—Emily ventured closer— "was *the family* . . . disturbed by my . . . my . . . ." She was unable to finish.

"I went to my room early as well, but I am certain your need for privacy was understood, considering the weight of the day's events," Miss DePeters assured her.

"It *was* difficult."

"I know."

Emily smiled softly. She faced the lean, solemn girl across the table, but suddenly she swayed, and seemed about to fall. The young woman rose to offer her assistance, but Emily was quickly in control of herself. "I only need some air," she said.

For a moment the two women studied each other.

"If you go up Temple Street," Miss DePeters said, "you will find a gate fairly hidden behind the lilacs. It leads to a small wood and a concealed glade just beyond. I tell the children it is where Indian spirits return so that they may, without evidence of the white man's hand, rendezvous with nature."

"Thank you. I shall go there."

Emily crossed to the kitchen door and then turned. The girl remained standing in the same position but her eyes had followed Emily, and her direct stare seemed powerful, wise, and tender at the same time. The red reflection of the kitchen fire shadowed her, and the silence was heavy between them. A damp log crackled and spat, hissed like an angry snake. Emily reached for the door handle feeling she must leave the room and Miss DePeters immediately.

"I will return for breakfast," she said. "No one need worry about my absence."

She nearly flew from the house, holding up her skirts as she made her way across the silvered grass and to the lilac grove. She found the gate, and only after reaching it, did she turn back for a moment to glance at the house. Then she walked cautiously through the profusion of trees, and after a very short time, entered the hidden glade.

Henry Murray's first marriage had been childless and he was in the fifth decade of his life before he became a father. Jerusha, his first-born, was his favorite though he would not have admitted it openly. She was also the quietest, and perhaps, the wisest. She sat now at the breakfast table at her father's right, straight and proud, and whispering under her breath, "Isaiah, Deborah . . ." whenever the younger children seemed to be remiss in their manners.

It was mandatory in the Murray household that all

be present at breakfast. Henry liked to have the sense of his entire family before he left them for the day. There was no question that, though fatherhood had been late in coming, Henry was a dedicated family man.

Emily had never sat at such a table. There had been three children in her own family, and not having servants or a governess in the house, they, too, had eaten all their meals together. But after her father had said Grace, silence had been observed. The squire had felt that conversation at mealtimes was bad for the digestion. Occasionally he had made comments, but no one except her mother had dared reply. And several times he had even lost his temper. Once he had crashed food and plate together into the fire because he had been served on a chipped plate. That same afternoon Emily took every chipped plate and glass from the shelves, went behind the barn so as not to disturb the household, and smashed them all. She was eleven years of age at the time.

"Miss DePeters has written a play about Pocahontas for us, and I am going to be Pocahontas," Jerusha was saying excitedly.

"I'm John Smith," Isaiah said.

"And I am Miles Standish." Deborah grinned devilishly as she spread a long wisp of her red hair beneath her nose.

Isaiah giggled and Jerusha looked sternly at him.

"Perhaps Miss DePeters can verify this," her father said seriously, "but I cannot recall that Miles Standish was a mustachioed fellow."

They all laughed, then turned to Miss DePeters, who sat between Isaiah and Deborah.

"I believe, sir, that fictional license is permissible in this case," she said softly.

"And anyway, Miles Standish wasn't a girl," Isaiah said. "And Deborah isn't a boy!"

"When is this performance to take place?" their father asked.

"At teatime," Deborah announced.

"Would you come, Father, please?" Jerusha pleaded.

"We will see, we will see," he said.

The children exchanged happy smiles. With their father, a reply like that was as good as a promise.

"Oh, dear," Chloe sighed. "Afternoon session at court might not be over by teatime." She glanced over to Emily.

"You must not miss the children's play on my account. We will, of course, leave early," Emily said.

"You are sure you won't mind?" Chloe's protectiveness and her woman's curiosity were obviously at odds.

"I am sure," Emily insisted.

Agnes appeared from the front hallway. "Mrs. Austin Dickinson has arrived. What shall I tell her?" she asked in a voice that Sue could not have helped hearing in the room just beyond.

Emily stood up. "Please do not disturb yourselves. My sister is here to see me. Perhaps you would be kind enough to allow us the use of the library for a few moments?" She excused herself and went immediately from the room.

Henry Murray smoked large cigars, and the library, which had not yet had its morning airing, still reeked of the smell of them. Sue turned up her nose, went to a window, and opened it wide. She was not used to cigars or to men like Henry Murray who smoked them. She breathed the fresh air deeply, as if her life depended upon its intake, before finally coming back into the room and closer to Emily. Perhaps no one knew Emily better than Sue, and she was aware that if she opened this conversation on the wrong foot, she would lose Emily's cooperation before she could broach the subject she had come to speak to her about.

"Perhaps it is an acquired smell," she said, her nose still twitching with the odor of the cigar.

Emily smiled.

Sue came closer and took her hands in her own. "Are you all right, Em?" she asked.

"Yes, quite."

"I read the *Republican* last night and found the report on the trial disturbing," Sue began.

"A murder trial could hardly be less."

"Everywhere you go they speak of it, and of the mysterious woman in black who sits in the courtroom."

"Yes, I have been thinking about that. It might be I chose too dramatic a disguise."

"Need you continue attending, Em?" It was said.

"No, but I shall do so anyway."

"Certainly you have had a fair opportunity to observe Judge Lord on the bench."

"It is not just that." Emily drew away. She could never convey to Sue her fascination with the trial itself, nor how important its outcome had come to mean to her.

Sue sat, weariness weighting her against her will. She had had very little sleep since coming to Springfield and there was too much on her mind. "Em," she said, knowing as she spoke that she should hold her tongue, "there are terrible problems between Austin and myself. I will not say that they are insurmountable, but they seem to be growing so." There was pain in Sue's face and a quiver to her lip.

Emily came immediately to her side. "Sue, darling, it will be all right. I know it will."

"It will never be the same. It can't. Emily, this will be difficult for you to accept, but I feel I must be truthful with you. I believe—I am quite sure—" it was difficult for Sue to complete the sentence—"Austin is . . . well, *interested* in another woman."

Emily spun away. "I cannot and will not believe that, Sue, and neither should you."

"It won't help me to be an ostrich about it. I think it is so, and that had it not been so, he would never have allowed me to come to Springfield. He would have come himself. Austin is not only an adulterer but a hypocrite as well, and you should take that into account yourself if he reacts badly to the situation between you and Otis Lord."

"I don't want to hear any more." Emily turned to leave.

"Em, if you want to experience life, you will have to face it. Not looking at it and not seeing it will keep it always outside you."

Emily turned, and seeing the exhaustion on Sue's fine, small face, came back to her side, helped her as she rose wearily from the chair, aware of how thin Sue was, of how she herself had been so wrapped up in her own problems and adventures, she had not noticed. "What can I do, Sue?" she asked gently.

"For Austin and me? Nothing. I have made it all too clear to Austin that the life he gives me does not fulfill me as a woman. The damage has been done. It would be, I guess, impossible for me to repair his ego, and as impossible for Austin to take steps to repair our marriage."

"You haven't made any plans?" Emily was alarmed.

"Only to remain here until you are ready to go home with me, and then to continue on for the children and for appearances' sake."

Emily's love and compassion for Sue were such that she sensed Sue's state of mind and wanted desperately to help her if help was needed. But on the other hand, she felt resentment that her world was not exactly as she believed it to be. "Why, Sue, why? Why tell me now?" she whispered.

"Because you mean a great deal to me, and because

to some extent I share with the rest of the Dickinsons the guilt for your naïveté. Such things as the true picture of my marriage have always been held back from you. That is why I could read last night's newspaper and become alarmed. I am certain that you are not prepared for this kind of exposure. And when I find that it has, indeed, sent you to hide in your room, I feel I have good reason to fear for your well-being. One step at a time, Em. Face the facts of our life, of yours, but, darling"—she paused and caught her breath and took Emily's hands in her own—"don't go back into that courtroom. I beg you. Stay in Springfield if you wish. Austin accepts my story. You are safe from him, and even if he should interfere, you now have the ammunition to stand up to him. Use the time to better advantage than paining yourself with the tragedy in that courtroom."

Emily felt the grip of Sue's hand, heard the insistence in her voice. Sue was frightened. Never before had Emily seen fear in that dearly loved face.

"Em, darling, please, please listen to me. Judge Lord is like any other man. He will want companionship, love, and, darling, a wife in the true sense. I suspect you also shut him out last night. Will he understand if the shock of the trial forces you to do it again? Don't go back. Spend the day with me. We can shop, or take a drive. For your own sake, Em, don't complicate things."

The ghosts returned and Emily could not sweep them away. "I cannot explain it, Sue," she replied with wide-eyed and childlike candor, "but I am compelled to go back. There are sounds in my attic and I must find out if I know who or what they belong to."

Silence came between them. Each was endeavoring to collect her thoughts, and each was moved strongly by concern for the other. It was Sue who left the room first, leaving Emily in the silent, vacant library where even the odor of Henry Murray's cigar had disappeared.

The day had begun for Judge Lord with two letters—one from Abbie and one from her mother, Mary. They had hardly put him in a good mood, with their recollections and reminders of the past. It would have been difficult to believe that the judge's past might contain buried and sheltered sorrows and shames. He seemed a singularly unblighted man whose only cross had been his wife's death. Yet for the judge, the past lingered like a soundless apparition in corners and passageways and doorways, and when suddenly met, would catapult him into mute confusion. Not that he rationally considered himself guilty of indiscretion— but, yes, the fact was, whenever he was surprised by the past he did suffer a strong, full measure of guilt.

It was difficult for him to separate his feelings well enough to see fully the direction of this guilt, but Elizabeth's family always regarded him with such high esteem that it caused him grievous pangs. It made him, for one thing, immeasurably uncomfortable that he—a man in his sixties who had so recently lost a wife—should be in pursuit of a younger woman and should be entertaining any carnal desires whatsoever. To compound his guilt, Emily had been a young woman he had known and desired while Elizabeth was alive, whom he had almost compromised those many years ago in Boston, and—he supposed—even now. It seemed to him that the sooner they were married, the sooner all these unpleasant ruminations would stop. Therefore, even burdened with this important trial, he viewed his courtship of Emily as his prime consideration.

He was extremely happy to see Henry Murray in his chambers before the day's session began. The two men greeted each other warmly and Henry wasted no time in explaining the reason for his visit.

"Now look, Otis," he began, "I'm not one for interfering in another man's life—and anyway, you are much too old a dog for anyone to retrain. But you have placed me, yes, and Chloe, too, in a damned difficult position." He was pacing the room, and he paused, finally, before a brass sculpture of the scales of justice. "Otis, this lady friend of yours is a very unique woman. I don't mean to imply that she is odd, but you must admit her reactions are a bit unusual."

"She has led a very cloistered life. You remember Edward Dickinson. Think how difficult it must have been to be his daughter."

"Be that as it may, Otis, she is like a delicate violin string drawn tauter than it can bear. She'll break, mind you, and I would not want to see that," he declared, turning and facing his friend. "Especially in my own home, Otis," he added.

"I spent a sleepless and restless night, Henry. I know. I *know.*"

"Well, damn it, man, what are you going to do?"

"I'm not sure, but I promise you, Emily will be fine. I will see to that."

Otis had committed himself—he had declared himself to be Emily's protector as well as her lover and he knew that Henry Murray would not allow him to forget it. The old friends stood facing each other, sunlight coming down on them through the high-arched windows. The issue was clear and they understood each other.

When Henry left, the questions roamed in the judge's mind like uneasy spirits. Should he insist that Emily return to Amherst? No! He could only protect her if he was by her side, if she never again locked him out as she had done the previous night. That had been a severe shock and he had been torn between the injury to his ego and his intense concern that he might be responsible for her further withdrawal from him and the world.

Well, he had committed himself to Henry, to Emily, and to himself. Emily would not break. He would see to that.

Mary's and Abbie's letters were on his desk and he ripped them to pieces and tossed them into a basket. The act raised his spirits and unleashed the old lion in him. When he was called to session he marched into the courtroom with such a proprietary air that glances were exchanged and both the prosecution and the defense wondered whether he had come into possession of facts they did not have.

"Your Honor," Mr. Waterman said, "I would like to call Miss Nora Griffin to the stand."

"Proceed."

The bailiff called out her name. A red-faced, nervous young woman in an ill-fitting dress and a hat of wilted flowers stepped forward. Maud Hagarty, from her gallery seat, looked down on her with grave disapproval. The young woman seemed aware of this and kept her eyes downward as she crossed to the witness stand. She did not raise her glance until after she had been duly sworn in.

"Miss Griffin," Mr. Waterman asked, "have you ever seen the two defendants before?"

"Yes, sir."

"Would you please tell the court the circumstances."

For a few moments Nora Griffin seemed unable to speak. She trembled noticeably and was staring out and up to the gallery.

"Is something the matter, Miss Griffin?" Judge Lord asked.

"No, sir. That is . . . your Honor."

"Are you able to continue?"

"Yes, your Honor."

"Then please proceed."

"Well, you see, I am in service of a family just down the street from the Kidder house and Maud Hagarty is a very special friend to me." She paused and looked up to the gallery, then bit her lip in a conscious effort to fight back tears.

"Go on, Miss Griffin," Mr. Waterman urged.

She let out a deep sigh before resuming. "Poor Maud is an orphan and I have loved her like a sister. She worked very long hours, very long, and it was always hard to get her to come out and join me in a bit of fun. Oh, I don't mean nothing unrespectable! Just a walk by Stearns's Park. Things like that. But Maud never would go, so most often I would have to go to the old gent's."

"Do you mean Mr. Kidder's house?"

"Yes, sir, Mr. Kidder's house. I'd have to go there to see Maud. I didn't make a habit of it, because I always respected it was her place of employ, but young Mr. Kidder was kind to me when I did come."

"Which brother was that, Miss Griffin?"

"Mr. Dwight. Mr. Charles was away a lot. I seldom saw him."

"But, in fact, you do know both defendants, do you not?"

"Oh, yes, sir."

"Have you ever seen them together?"

"Yes, sir. As I said, I would stop by from time to time to visit Maud. One time—"

"When was this, Miss Griffin?"

"Oh, a year ago. February, I recall. There was snow on the ground and I had received a valentine that I wanted to show Maud." She giggled and shaded her face for a moment to hide her embarrassment. "I'm sorry, sir."

"What time of day was it?"

"It wasn't day, sir. It was evening. I had finished up the supper dishes before I left my own employ."

"Please continue, Miss Griffin."

"I came to the rear door and I heard these awful shouts—such a carry-on! Shameful language, too! There was nothing to be done about overhearing it neither, as it come from the old gent's—ah—Mr. Kidder's room, and that is over the kitchen."

"Was the window opened?"

"Yes, it was, and fact be, that was what the fighting was about. I looked up and there was Mr. Charles before the opened window holding it fast in that position, and there was Mr. Dwight right behind him."

"You could see both of them quite clearly, could you?"

"Yes, sir. There was a bright moon and the lights was up in the room as well."

"And though you seldom saw Mr. Charles, and he was an identical twin to Mr. Dwight, you were able to tell them immediately apart?"

"It was easy as pie, sir. It was the way they was dressed. The man at the window wore a ruffled shirt and his hair was groomed all fancy-like. The man behind him had his hair terrible unruly and wore a leather vest that I seen on Mr. Dwight many times. No doubting, sir, it was Mr. Charles at the window and Mr. Dwight behind him."

"And you would swear on the Bible that you could see them *both* quite clearly?"

"Oh, yes. They stood at an angle sort of from where I be. I could see them both as good as I can see them now."

"Proceed."

She tossed her head back and placed her hands on her hips. " 'What kind of a damned-fool thing is that to do!' Mr. Dwight was shouting," she said, lowering her hands. "Well, excuse me, sir, I would never say such a thing, but those was Mr. Dwight's very words."

"The court excuses you, Miss Griffin. Do continue."

"Then they exchanged some very high words, sir."

"Can you recall what they were?"

"Well . . . Mr. Charles says, 'It stinks of decay in here!' And Mr. Dwight says, 'A chill could kill him.' And Mr. Charles says, 'If it does, maybe I won't be forced to!' Mr. Dwight then come alongside him. 'Shut up! He can hear you!' he says. And Mr. Charles answers, shouting it, 'Good! Good! Hear that, old man! Die, damn you, die!' "

There was a shocked gasp from the spectators, as though all those listening were one.

"Sorry, sir, but those were his words."

"Continue, Miss Griffin."

"Well, then there was a scuffle at the window. Mr. Dwight was trying to close the window and Mr. Charles was holding it opened. Maud come to the kitchen door then, though I didn't think that she had heared me with all that commotion. She looked . . . well . . . distracted.

Very nettled. And I put me arm about her shoulders and we goes into the house, the kitchen, that is, together."

"Did Miss Hagarty wear a shawl, as though she were, in fact, planning an outing?"

"No, sir, she was just distracted, as I says, and was just running from the house to get away from all that fuss, I guess."

"So you went into the kitchen together, is that correct?"

"Yes, sir, and the kettle was up and some apple pie on the table and I thought it might unruffle Maud if she had something to fill her stomach."

"Didn't you tell the court it was after supper?"

"Yes, it was, but Maud makes very good apple pie."

There was polite laughter in the court.

"Continue, Miss Griffin."

"So I went to prepare some tea. But there was such terrible noises overhead—it was the old gent's room, as I said, up there—and Maud begun to cry. Well, I didn't know what to do, but it comes to me that Maud shouldn't have to listen to all that rattle upstairs, so I says, 'Let's take the tea and the pie and go into the sewing room.' That's where Maud did the sewing and the ironing and we often chewed a bit in there. She agreed, and so we goes out into the front hallway—the sewing room being on the other side of the house downstairs—Maud leading and me carrying the refreshments.

"Well, just as we entered the hallway, Mr. Charles, with Mr. Dwight just behind him, come down the stairway shouting something terrible at each other. Maud and me stepped into the shadows so they wouldn't see us. Mr. Charles says, 'I don't know why I bother to come back!' And Mr. Dwight says, 'Because he's your father and this is your home.' 'Damned if it is!' Mr. Charles shouts. 'Please be quiet, Charles,' Mr. Dwight begs.

They was now at the foot of the stairs and facing each other and Mr. Dwight had Mr. Charles by the shoulder. 'You're an ass, Dwight,' Mr. Charles says, and then he raised his voice even more. 'He should be taken out and shot!' Then Mr. Charles pushed Mr. Dwight's hand off his shoulder.

" 'He knows full well what he's doing, Dwight,' Mr. Charles says, 'robbing you of your best years, your right to live a life of your own. He's made you into a nurse-maid, made himself *appear* more helpless than he is—all to keep you here by his side. He has no right, Dwight. But I can see you haven't got the guts to do anything about it. I keep coming back just to see if I can bring you to your senses. He belongs in an institution. And you belong among the living!' Then Mr. Charles started for the front door and Mr. Dwight followed.

" 'Don't go this way,' Mr. Dwight says. 'I have to leave this house and you, Dwight,' Mr. Charles says, 'before I puke at the self-pity and the self-abuse and stink and decay in it!' Well, then Mr. Dwight grabbed his arm to hold him back from leaving, and Mr. Charles *swings* —oh, my, I never saw nothing like it! He swings power-ful hard and hit Mr. Dwight a blow on the side of his head and then hard again in the stomach." She winced in pain, and the courtroom with her. "And then Mr. Dwight went reeling. Well, it was all confusion then, because Maud screamed and I dropped the tray and we goes running over to where Mr. Dwight was *laid out.*"

"Are you saying that Dwight Kidder was uncon-scious?"

"Cold as a dead fish. We could hear the old gent ring the bell beside his bed. 'Mr. Kidder heard it all,' Maud says. And Mr. Charles says, 'Good! Good!' But Maud looked so fearful that he told her to go up to his father, and then Mr. Charles sent me for some cold water and clean cloths, and when I come back he had Mr. Dwight sitting up in his arms. 'No need for that now,' Mr. Charles says. 'Fetch me some hot water instead and some disinfectant.' He was helping Mr. Dwight to his feet as I run from the room. It took me some time to find where the disinfectant was. When I returned they was both in the parlor, so I went there. Mr. Dwight was resting on the settee and Mr. Charles was standing beside him. 'Leave those things, Nora,' he says, 'and if you value your friendship with Maud, say nothing about this to anyone.' "

"He threatened you, then?"

"You might say so, sir."

"And did you leave, Miss Griffin?"

"I had no other choice, sir."

"Well, thank you, Miss Griffin. The court knows this has been most painful for you, and we appreciate it. Your witness, Mr. Leonard."

Nora Griffin shifted nervously at the stand.

"Would you like some water, Miss Griffin?" Judge Lord inquired.

"Oh, yes, sir. I would indeed."

The bailiff brought a glass of water to her and the courtroom waited breathlessly while she satisfied her thirst.

"Now, Miss Griffin," Mr. Leonard began, "you have told this court that the events you have just described took place shortly after Valentine's Day last year. That would make it approximately fourteen and one half months ago, is that correct?"

"I ain't much on numbers, sir, but I trust you be."

"You may take my word, Miss Griffin, it is approximately fourteen and one half months. A short time relatively, and yet quite a long span to carry in one's mind such a detailed memory of events and conversation. Do you usually have such extraordinary recall?"

"It was vivid, it was. And violent."

"Have you never been audience to family quarrels before?"

"Me own, o' course."

"And do you recall those quarrels as verbatim?"

"Verbatim?"

"Exactly as they were."

"No, sir. And they was not quarreling that night. They was fighting."

"I will rephrase the question. How is it possible that you could memorize in such small detail a fight between two men who had nothing whatsoever to do with your life?" Mr. Leonard glanced over to the jury as though sharing his disbelief with them.

" 'Cause, sir, in me own family, me brothers was always cuffing each other and me father cuffing them. No one meant bad by it. It was just the way things was, sir. But in houses like the Kidders' or me own employ, well, that was different, sir. It was something shocking, you see for *them* to cuff each other. And the things Mr. Charles said about the old gent—it be shocking, sir, coming as it was from *them.* "

"Well, Miss Griffin, since your memory of the fight that night is so extraordinary, perhaps there are other things that were said at that time that you could remember if you set your mind to it."

"I think that was about all there was to it, sir."

"Well, did you leave the house immediately upon Mr. Charles's' request that you do so?"

"I left the place where he was, sir."

"But not the house?"

"No, sir."

"You disobeyed his order?"

"Yes, sir. But you see, I was worried fierce about

Maud. So instead of leaving the house just then, I went to her room, which was behind the kitchen, and waited for her to return."

"How long did you wait?"

"It seemed very long, but I can't say for sure how long. I was worried fierce, as I says."

"What happened when Miss Hagarty did return?"

"Well, it surprised me. I'll never understand a person's ingratitude, sir."

"I repeat, Miss Griffin, what happened when Miss Hagarty returned to her room and found you waiting there?"

"She was angry. She told me to go, and in very harsh words!"

"Were any other exchanges made?"

"Some."

"Well, come, come, Miss Griffin, a young lady with your great talent for remembering details must certainly recall what preceeded such a good friend's angry words and induced that anger."

" 'You shouldn't be here. Please go,' she says. And I says, 'Maudie-love, this is me, old Nora, and I want you to know you got a friend.' And she says, 'If you be me friend, you'll go!' And I answers, 'If you be smart, you'll go yourself with me!' " She paused then and cast a slightly brazen smile up to the gallery.

"Continue, Miss Griffin."

"Well, she turned away then. 'Please go!' she says. 'They's common and dangerous,' I tells her. That's when she turns on me. 'I knew you wouldn't be understanding,' she says, and there was a mean look in her eyes, and tears as well. 'I understand, I do,' I tells her. 'They got murder in their soul. The devil's got hold of them.' Then she pushed me! 'Nora Griffin,' she says, 'if the devil's got them, it's got me too, 'cause they be all I have that's family. It's love for each other that has them caught up so tightlike, and the likes of you wouldn't be understanding!' "

"What did you reply?"

"I know me manners and have me pride. I said nothing more and I left."

"And have you seen Maud Hagarty since that evening?"

"No, sir."

"Do I understand you to say that you have not seen or exchanged letters with a friend you profess to love like a sister, for fourteen and one half months, when she resides not half a block from your place of employ?"

"That's right, sir."

"Then you have been very angry with Miss Hagarty all this time?"

"I have that!"

"And are you still angry with her?"

"It was her that flung the words and her who should apologize."

"And how do you feel about Mr. Dwight and Mr. Charles, Miss Griffin?"

"They still be in the grip of the devil."

"Do you think it possible that they might be responsible for Miss Hagarty's attitude toward you?"

"I do that!"

"Well, thank you, Miss Griffin. I appreciate your cooperation."

Mr. Leonard turned away and returned to the defense table.

"Step down, Miss Griffin," Judge Lord said.

*E*arly in the afternoon there
had been a brief, sharp shower. The ground was still
damp. Raindrops clung to wet twigs and glistened on the
tips of the young green leaves. Emily sat waiting for Otis
Lord in the Murray library. The windows were closed
and a wood fire burned in the hearth. Day was almost
gone, but she made no effort to light the lamps.

Last night she had turned Otis away. Today had
been beautiful solely because she had given it to him. She
had sat in court studying his every move, his every gesture. She had come away with her head filled with im-
pressions of him and her heart with a yearning to feel his
touch, his presence so close that his breath would warm
her.

Now she feared he might grow too dear, that language might be done between them, that such a love as
she felt this moment might be speechless and so seem to
withhold.

A strange light fell across the room. Its appearance
was unexpected and startling. "Eden," she thought,
"ebbs away to diviner Edens." She rose and went to the
window and stared into the arc of light as into the flames

of a fire, and in the same way, she seemed transfixed, mesmerized by the brilliance. So taken was she that she did not hear him rap upon the door, or the door open, or close, or his footsteps as they approached. But suddenly she turned, and as she did, the light failed and they stood facing each other in the fire-warmed semidark.

"I would have come out of Eden to open the door for you if I had known you were there," she said. Even in the dimness of the light he could see a smile come to her face. "You must knock," she jested, "as Gabriel does —with a trumpet, I suppose."

Then they were in each other's arms, and she clung to him. He was overwhelmed, incapable of moving, and stood holding her to him, looking out into the darkening garden.

It was a long time before either of them spoke. But finally each whispered the other's name and then they drew apart as though to hold their emotion close to themselves.

When he had come up the front path to the Murray house, Otis had keenly felt the presence of Emily as she had been when she was young, when they had been in Boston. The very strong sensation of that girl's presence had been by his side and had accompanied him up the front steps and across the hall to the library. At the door she had stood beside him, insistent, not to be turned away. "Otis, I am here," the young Emily seemed to whisper in his ear. "I have not vanished from your life. I am here."

"We should make plans," he said to the real woman.

"My heart has lived alone for so many years, Otis, it is conditioned to independence and, I am afraid, committed elsewhere at times. That will not make you suffer, will it?" She turned away from him, as though afraid of his answer.

But he pulled her to him and made her face him

again. "Emily, you must stop looking so deep inside yourself. You are blinding yourself to exterior wonders." His voice grew solemn. "Don't make the path to your heart so difficult that others cannot find their way there," he said.

She was startled by this remark and by the intensity of Otis' voice. "Otis, are you saying that I am making the way difficult for you?"

He stood there a little awkwardly, unsmiling, his manner an odd mixture of tenderness and reprimand. "Perhaps I only fear that you *might*," he said seriously.

She was grateful for the shadows of early evening that were so heavy in the room, as they gave her some sense of distance between them. In order to be objective, to understand the full significance of what Otis was saying and what she was feeling, such distance was necessary.

Otis was not a man who accepted things lightly. He was critical of himself and of others as well. But it was not so much what he said but what he withheld that marked him for the man of stature he was. He was an original, not an eccentric, whose rationality governed him and forced him to live in a sorted, sifted, arranged world. Their interlude in Boston had been the most eccentric incident in his life, and bringing her here to Springfield, the only lapse in his rationality. It proved that he loved her mightily, and also that he would be a man always to have the last word.

Day faded completely. They were now in darkness. The room was solemnly still but there was an extraordinary static in the air.

"Don't allow yourself to put off our future together," he said with a simplicity that touched her.

"I desire our future with as much immediacy as you do," she replied, her voice trembling in spite of all her efforts to control it. He cut a path through the darkness and stood over her. "There are though," she continued timidly, conscious of his nearness, "some bridges to be spanned, some cases to be settled first."

"There is your mother, of course." He might have been addressing a courtroom except for the tender glance he gave her. "But Lavinia remains at home and Austin and Sue are near at hand. I shall, of course, insist upon contributing my aid in securing and paying for a nurse-companion."

"Is that solution fair to Vinnie?"

"Is it fair to us, otherwise?" He maintained his self-control, but his tone of voice had become more personal.

"No, no . . . it is not." She turned aside, embarrassed at having to deal with practicalities. "Where shall we live?" she asked quietly.

"Salem, of course."

"And Abbie and Mary Farley?"

"That is up to you."

"We cannot turn them out."

"I am well able to provide a second home for them," he assured her.

She was staring at him now and the reflection of the flames danced in her eyes, making her golden in its glow. "You have thought of everything," she said.

"I have thought of nothing but you and our finally being united," he replied.

Her thoughts coursed back through the years—all dimly lighted now, pathless, strange-looking, cloaked as it seemed in the dreariness of winter—*years without Otis*. What a long journey she had taken. Dull gleams of memory passed through her mind, of expectations and disappointments, fitful images only, once seeming like life and death itself, now only trifles. Visions of a future with Otis eclipsed all else. There was no need to regret now —that was all over.

"We can make plans a week or two after my return

to Amherst," she finally replied. "I want to tell Vinnie and Mother myself—and Austin as well. Is that agreeable?" She asked it submissively, her voice soft, her manner shy.

"My instinct says *Don't let any more time elapse,* but rationality forces me to say yes," he answered, the words ponderous but his tone light.

He was not prepared for her next action, for as she threw her arms about his neck, he almost lost his balance. She laughed but did not release her hold.

"I don't think I will find enough devices to live till we can be together!" she said, and her face was bright with happiness.

"You look very beautiful this moment, Emily," he told her gravely.

She still held onto him but drew her head back so that she could study his face. "I don't believe anyone ever called me beautiful before," she told him quietly, her shyness returning.

The fire had reached its peak and the room was growing very warm. "Emily," he whispered. "Emily." He pulled her close to him. He could feel her body against his own. "Oh, my God, Emily, how can you forgive me?" he cried and kissed her lips and found them as feverish as his own. They clung together and her passion seemed equally strong.

"I don't think it is a thing to forgive," she said, and pressed her lips once more against his.

Finally he was able to hold her away from him. "I do not know how well you understand these things, Emily, but I think one of us must leave this room." He took her hand and went before her to the door. "Would you do me the honor of dining with me tomorrow evening, Miss Dickinson?" he asked. "If you desire to remain unrevealed to Springfield society, we can dine in my rooms. I promise you, dear Emily, the greatest propriety shall prevail."

She smiled up at him. "My answer is *yes*, and my only comment is on the sham and coldness of propriety." She glanced immediately away and placed her hand on the door handle, withdrawing it as quickly. "The door, Otis," she reminded him in a supremely feminine voice.

"Yes, yes, of course."

He opened it to let her pass and stood watching her as she crossed the hallway to the front parlor with a sureness of gait and pride of bearing he had not been aware of before.

*The farthest Thunder that I heard*
*Was nearer than the Sky*
*And rumbles still, though torrid Noons*
*Have lain their missiles by—*
*The Lightning that preceded it*
*Struck no one but myself—*
*But I would not exchange the Bolt*
*For all the rest of Life—*

# 21

$\mathcal{C}$harles Kidder had a smile that even on the witness stand took its own immediate charm for granted. It was difficult, in fact, to imagine any other man in his position having so comfortable and casual an air. Yet, the finely sharpened intelligence in his eyes denied one's first impression. Charles Kidder was a young man who missed very little of what went on around him, who experienced much of what he contemplated and contemplated quite ruthlessly all he experienced.

Though in his physiognomy there was little to set him apart from his twin, in attitude he was so totally different as to make each seem the antonym of the other. Whereas Dwight Kidder had the look of a young man who if married would succumb to his wife; if a father, to his child; or as a master, to his servant—Charles had that quality of daring spirit which comes from a certain hardness of heart. And whereas Dwight had an aura of servility that was the kind brought on by continual aversion to the giving of pain, by a softness which made the agony of others his, Charles wore a note of authority in a near-military manner.

There was a look of fear in Dwight Kidder's eyes as he glanced up to see his brother on the stand, as if he was unable to bear Charles to be in such a painful situation. Or, perhaps, he so dreaded the thought of his own future appearance before the court that he assumed it must be the same for his brother.

Charles was not without high purpose or courage. By his performance in the court he hoped to give Dwight a standard to follow. But so unlike were they that Dwight seemed, even now, to be suffering an acute spasm. He held his arms close about his body, as though in the grip of pain, and with silent, stuttering lips appeared to be chanting a prayer.

"Now, Mr. Kidder," Mr. Waterman was saying to Charles, "would you be kind enough to tell the court when you first left your father's house and the circumstances thereof?"

"I would be happy to do so, but I think, with the court's forbearance, there is something I would like to relate first." He turned away from Mr. Waterman and sought the judge's approval with the air of a keen and sincere petitioner. Charles Kidder was also not a young man who would waste energy in pandering to another man's vanity.

"I am afraid courtroom procedure must be respected, Mr. Kidder," the judge told him. "You must reply to Mr. Waterman's questions. But if you feel there is information that would assist this court in understanding the case to the fullest, then, before your own attorney questions you, the court will grant you a short recess from the stand so that you two may confer."

Charles muttered his appreciation and turned back to face his inquisitor.

"Shall I repeat the question?" Mr. Waterman asked.

"No, you inquired as to the night I first left home. I recall it quite clearly," Charles acknowledged. "It was the seventeenth of May, 1877. It would have been the sixteenth of May, except no night train left for Boston and I had to sit the entire night in the depot waiting for the first morning train. I was nineteen at the time."

"May the court assume you left your father's house in a state of agitation?"

"They certainly may! We had had a violent disagreement."

"Violent, Mr. Kidder?"

"Yes, Mr. Waterman—*violent*. We had verbally exchanged hostilities, you might say, and laid a great many things in the open. Neither of us physically touched the other. But, yes, there was violence between us."

"You were, I take it, exceedingly rude and disrespectful to your father?"

"Exceedingly."

Mr. Waterman's eyebrows arched and his nose appeared to lengthen. "Your mother died, I understand, when you and your brother were only nine years of age. Is that correct?"

"It is."

"And your father raised you, being both mother and father to you, giving you a church background, a comfortable home, and a superior edcuation. Is that correct, Mr. Kidder?"

"It is not, Mr. Waterman."

Mr. Waterman appeared shocked. "You received none of these things?" he inquired harshly.

"In my eyes, I did not. First, Mr. Waterman, no one could take the place of my mother, who was a gentle lady, a woman of great poetry of soul, leastways my father. Second, no one person can give another a church background. The person must belong to the church in spirit, which I never did. As to your third point, I might concede that my father gave me a comfortable home if you mean by that the homely comforts of a roof, food, and so forth. But if, as I suspect, your question means a home filled with love and a sense of protection—the answer is *no*. My father was incapable of love or understanding unless it was of his own persuasion. He only knew how to possess and only cared truly about *possessing*. Regarding a superior education, my father raised and educated both Dwight and myself to follow in his *murderous* footsteps, and when I sought an education of a broader and more humane nature, he refused. The education he gave me was in my opinion not superior to Maud Hagarty's education. She was, at least, trained up in the heart to be her own true self. My father would never permit that. Guns were his only true love. Guns and the money gotten by their manufacture."

"I don't believe we need go into that now, Mr. Kidder. The court is aware that your father earned his livlihood through the auspices of Smith and Wesson. Springfield's last census acknowledges over 36,000 inhabitants, approximately 6,000 of whom are employed by Smith and Wesson, gun manufacturers. That would mean, Mr. Kidder, that nearly one out of every six Springfield residents is in the employ of his firm. Are you, therefore, calling 6,000 of our finest citizens *murderers?*"

"I am."

"I see," said Mr. Waterman brusquely. He turned away from the witness stand and to the jury box. "On the evening in question, what was it you and your father exchanged such violent words about, Mr. Kidder?"

"My father had been ill and unable to carry on his business. He wanted Dwight and myself to carry on for him."

"What was your response?"

"The only civilized one there could be. I refused."

"You refused, Mr. Kidder, knowing the business

was your father's life and had been the means by which you and your brother had been cared for all your lives! I find that shocking."

"Not as shocking, I am sure, as the realization was to me when I learned, or rather, came to understand, the nature of my father's business!"

"Your father was a leather-man, was he not, Mr. Kidder?"

"My father made gun holsters. Nothing else. Just holsters for guns. That is quite an art, you know. A gun must be able to slip perfectly from a holster, must hang at just the right angle, must feel comfortable when a man is preparing for murder."

"Young man, it is you and your brother who are on trial here for murder, not the arms industry! I am afraid I must remind you and this court—to bring things around to their proper perspective—that Smith and Wesson supply the American Army with weapons now as they did during Indian uprisings and during times of war. As well, they supply watchmen and prison guards and isolated farm homes with protection. *Protection*, Mr. Kidder, not murder—*protection*. Now, you were saying that you refused your father's plea to come to his aid . . ."

"I said nothing of the sort. My father was a well-to-do man. Neither Dwight nor I wanted his blood money. He had enough to take care of his own needs for the rest of his life. Smith and Wesson was offering to buy him out. Only my father's ego and pride were at stake. I refused to pander to them. I told him I wanted no part of any profit that came from blood and death. I told him Dwight and I were fully capable of making our own way. He looked at me with a strange gleam in his eye. He hated me. I knew it that moment and was aware why he hated me. It was a piteous thing. I had his strength and he hated me for it, whereas Dwight had our mother's weakness and he loved Dwight for that. 'Dwight is not going anywhere with you!' he said, and there was something so gloating in his face that I was appalled and remember feeling a cold wetness creep down my back."

"What was your brother's reply?"

"He was frightened. Father had always terrified him. He said, 'I'll stay, Charles. It's all right. I'll stay.'" There were tears starting in Charles Kidder's eyes, but almost immediately his face stiffened and his eyes cleared. "My brother is a pacifist, but of another nature from myself."

"Did you leave then?"

"No, I did not. I said I would not depart without Dwight, and that if Dwight remained I would remain as well, to fight for what I believed to be right." A smile forced its way across his stiff lips. "The old man fairly erupted," he said in a voice suddenly terribly alive. "He started screaming wildly at me, and when he saw that I was unmovable, he turned to Dwight. 'Do you know what he is doing?' he shouted. 'Turning you against me!'"

"Did you consider that he might be right?"

"To turn away fear is a positive action. Dwight did not love Father, he feared him."

"That is your opinion, Mr. Kidder, an opinion founded on hot emotions and self-interest."

Charles Kidder smiled in a more relaxed manner. "Well, as I said, I had inherited a few qualities from my father."

"Let us hope that is so, Mr. Kidder, for your father held a position of earned respect in this community." Mr. Waterman walked away disdainfully and stood by his table. There was now a considerable distance between himself and the witness stand, so that he had to raise his voice for Charles Kidder to hear him. Doing so also insured that the spectators in the courtroom could now hear him equally well. "Did you or did you not remain, Mr. Kidder?"

"I stood my ground and refused to leave without Dwight."

"What happened then?"

"My father kept a gun on his body at all times. He went for it."

Mr. Waterman paled. "You are under oath, Mr. Kidder," he reminded him.

"I am quite aware of that. My father pointed his gun at me," he continued, "and told me to leave the house. 'If I don't, would you shoot me?' I asked. He told me he would, and I believed him. I turned to go. Then I heard this inhuman cry, like a drowning monkey. I turned back. My father was sprawled on the floor. I told Dwight not to touch him. 'He's ill, maybe dying,' Dwight said. I asked him, 'Dwight, did you make to follow me just now?' He nodded his head. Then he bent over the old man, and as he did so he told me to fetch the doctor. I did. I sent him back, but I did not return with him."

"You went directly to the train depot, is that correct?"

"It is."

"And discovered there was no train to Boston that night, is that correct?"

"Correct."

"Did you, in any manner, send word to find out how your father was during the night, or even if he had survived his stroke?"

"I did not."

"I find that appalling and am quite certain the court does as well, Mr. Kidder!"

"Objection!" Mr. Leonard called out.

"Sustained," the judge immediately agreed.

"I apologize, your Honor. I am afraid I was overcome."

For a moment Mr. Waterman appeared somewhat disconcerted. He removed the pince-nez from his nose and rubbed his eyes wearily before replacing them. Then he slowly advanced across the courtroom and stood directly facing the witness. "What did you do to earn your living in Boston, Mr. Kidder?"

"I was a professional gambler."

"At nineteen years of age." Mr. Waterman shook his head sadly. "Were there no honest trades for you to enter with your educational background?"

"I was and am an honest professional gambler, Mr. Waterman."

"Had you gambled before you left Springfield, either professionally or otherwise?"

"All of life is a gamble."

"I ask you to confine yourself to direct answers. Had you gambled before you left Springfield, professionally or otherwise?"

"I had."

"Was it professionally?"

"No."

"Then I take it you were gambling with your father's money, is that correct?"

Charles Kidder was slow in replying, and when he did, his voice was hard. "I was. It seemed somehow fit."

"Had you, in fact, had bad debts that your father, as a man of honor, paid for you?"

"As a man of insufferable pride he had."

"Had you also been remanded only weeks before your departure from home for being found drunk and disorderly on the streets of Springfield?"

"I was remanded because, when accosted by a policeman while taking an evening stroll, I told him to drop his gun and to fight like a man."

"Had you been drinking?"

"I had."

"And who paid your fine?"

"My father. I did not, however, ask him to do so and I never accepted a penny from him after that."

"I take it, then, that you went to Boston penniless. Is that how it was?"

"I borrowed money from Dwight."

"Was your brother self-supporting?"

"No, not at that time. My father gave him an allowance."

Mr. Waterman seemed to be considering something very carefully. He shifted his mountainous weight and rested his chin on his hand. "Have you been a professional gambler for all the years since, Mr. Kidder?"

"I told this court so when I was sworn in. Yes, Mr. Waterman, I have been."

"At any time in those years have you had to borrow money from your brother?"

"I have."

"Yes . . . yes, you have, and I put it to you, Mr. Kidder, that those times, those times you needed money for pressing gambling debts, were the only times you returned to see your brother and father. And I put it to you further that you took money from your brother *knowing* it came from your father. And I put it to you further still that immediately after receiving the funds you needed you would depart again. Is that not correct?"

"At twenty-one my brother and myself came into a small inheritance from my mother's family estate. It was from those funds that I borrowed."

"What had happened to *your* inheritance?"

"I had spent it."

"Do you mean spent or *lost* it, Mr. Kidder?"

"Both."

"All right, Mr. Kidder, now, if you will, I would like you to tell the court the circumstances of your return to your father's house on the night of his grievous assault and death. Did you return that night to borrow money from your brother Dwight?"

"I did."

"What time of day did you arrive in Springfield?"

"It was afternoon. I came in on the five-fifteen."

"Strange, I cannot recall a train at five-fifteen in the afternoon from Boston."

"I arrived from New York. I had been there on business."

"The court quite understands."

"Damn it! The court does not understand!"

"Mr. Kidder," the judge warned, "I am certain you would not want me to penalize you for being in contempt of this court."

"I am sorry, your Honor, but—" Charles began, and then, after glancing over to Mr. Leonard, who was about to object, was silent.

Mr. Waterman stood calmly, not moving, not even shifting his weight to the other foot. "Were you expected home?" he asked.

"No, I was not."

"Who greeted you?"

"No one. The house appeared empty. I called out but no one replied. I went into the kitchen but Maud was not there. I left a package I had brought for her on the kitchen table and went upstairs. Dwight came out of Father's room to greet me. He looked as though he had just been aroused from sleep, and was still exhausted. We had only exchanged greetings when Father called out for us to come in. Once we were in the room he said nothing to me but waited until we were by the bed. Then he propped himself up on his pillows and took Dwight by the arm. 'So your brother has come home,' he said. 'Hello, Father,' I greeted him, and then, seeing how poorly Dwight appeared in the clearer light, asked him if he was all right. He told me he had been up most of the night with Father, but as Father did not like to be alone, and it was Maud's off day, he had spent it by Father's side. He had had very little sleep in the previous twenty-four hours. I asked Dwight to come down to the kitchen with me to prepare the supper trays. Actually, I wanted to speak to him alone.

"Father objected, but Dwight pacified him by telling him we would only be gone a few moments. When we were in the kitchen he told me Father had been having these ghastly nightmares and that he had become fearful of sleep. 'He feels like a murderer!' I told Dwight. And I added, 'Thank the Lord he will have had some suffering before he dies!' "

There had been an awed and fascinated silence in the courtroom until Charles Kidder's last statement. Now there was a stirring and low voices and the whirring of women's hand-fans.

"Order, order," the judge called.

Mr. Waterman looked out over the courtroom and toward the jury with dismay. Liza Goodlift had quickly and immediately stifled a short gasp and the foreman had turned his glance toward Dwight to see how he had taken his brother's blasphemous words. Dwight sat with head bowed, eyes downcast. Mr. Leonard fought desperately to catch Charles's eye, but finally, unable to do so, sat back grimly.

At the rear of the courtroom Chloe, fearing the proceedings might be too much for Emily, turned to her with outstretched hand, as though expecting Emily to be in a swoon. Emily was not. She was perched on the edge of the bench and was frozen in attention. Chloe leaned back, and fluttering her fan close to her face, waited expectantly for the next moment of drama.

"How long was it before you returned to your father's room?" Mr. Waterman continued.

"Five, ten minutes, perhaps. I helped Dwight with laying the trays. Maud had prepared and left a cold roast."

"During that time what did you and your brother discuss?"

"His lack of freedom during all the years he cared for my father."

"Did you discuss anything else?"

"I tried once more to convince him to come away with me."

"Were you successful?"

"No. I knew then that only my father's death would release Dwight."

There was another rustle throughout the courtroom.

"So you finally returned to your father's room together with the trays?"

"Together, but not with the trays. We both heard a scream coming from his room and ran up to discover what the matter was."

"What had happened, Mr. Kidder?"

"My father was lying on the floor by the side of his bed. At first I thought he had fallen out of bed, but his position was wrong. Though he supposedly was not able to stand, it seemed he must have done so. For that matter, he had obviously stood and taken several steps from the bed to where he had collapsed. The drawer was opened next to the bed and it was empty. There was always a small handgun there. On close inspection I saw the gun poking from underneath his body."

"Was he unconscious?"

"No, he was in pain and he was angry."

"Did he speak?"

Charles Kidder laughed. "Vehemently," he said.

"What did he say?"

"He was shrieking about a new will. He had threatened he would write a new will on each of my visits. Dwight and I lifted him between us and put him back on the bed. He was holding his gun against his chest and he refused to relinquish it. For a few moments he lay gasping, with his head resting back on the pillows. Dwight took a tablet from a bottle and tried to force him to take one.

" 'Ease your mind, write your will,' I told him. 'I have told you over and over again, I want none of your money. You are an accomplice in slaughter, and for my peace and my soul, I want no part of it.' He lay there, withered, his clawlike hand nuzzling his gun against his shrunken chest. 'For you,' he wheezed, 'for you.' Then the black pits of his eyes closed and we thought he might be dead, but before either of us had touched him to feel his pulse, he opened his eyes again and even managed to prop himself up. Before he spoke again, Dwight began to explain to me that Father wanted to rewrite the will to leave me the business interests and Dwight the house. Ha had been talking about it all night and all day. I started to laugh.

" 'Laugh,' my father gasped, 'but I will leave you my curse whether you want it or not.'

" 'I won't help you write your will and neither will Dwight. Your curse will go with you wherever you go!' I shouted. I don't know what made me say such a mad thing. I believe in no *other world*, or curses either! He had just infuriated me to that point.

"I thought I had better leave before I said anything more and I turned away from him and started toward the door. The fire was dying and the light of day had passed and the room was filled with the smell of decay. I will never forget that. The smell. 'Charles!' he screamed in a cracking and high-pitched voice. I kept going. 'I will kill you first!' he gasped. I heard Dwight call out in a restraining fashion, 'Father!' and then there was the sound of a body falling, and I whirled. Dwight had dropped to the floor, fearing the worst, that Father would shoot him to keep him from leaving with me.

"There Father stood beside the bed, grasping the bedpost with one bony fist and pointing the gun at Dwight with the other. It all had a very unreal quality. The room was bathed in a strange red light from the fire and he stood in a white nightdress, looking like some exhumed corpse. I took a step toward him and he immediately shifted his aim and raised the barrel of the gun to a position level with my chest.

"Out of the corner of my eye I saw Dwight crawling toward him. Then Dwight reached out and grabbed his leg and they were both down. The gun went off and I ran over to them. Dwight drew away first, and blood covered his chest. I thought he had been shot. Then I realized the blood was not his and that it was Father who had been wounded.

"He was moaning, but the shot was not fatal. It had struck his shoulder. I yelled that I would fetch the doctor and started to run out. My back was turned when I heard the second gunshot. When I turned back, Father was in a heap on the floor. I could not see the gun. Later, of course, I discovered it was beneath his body."

"Had you heard anything at all in those few moments?"

"Perhaps a gasp. Nothing else."

Mr. Waterman breathed heavily. "You are, then, telling this court that you had nothing at all to do with those two gunshots. Is that it, Mr. Kidder?"

"Phrased that way, yes, I guess that is so."

"You are also telling this court that you stood by and allowed your brother to knock down a man as infirm as your father. Frankly, Mr. Kidder, I am personally disgusted and morally offended."

"Your Honor—" Mr. Leonard began.

"I apologize, your Honor," Mr. Waterman added instantly, "but I had a vision that moment of that shriveled and dying old gentleman, wounded and bleeding like a helpless child and sprawled between his own two sons—one who had shot him and one who did nothing to intervene. I found the story that was being told, that Charles Kidder had none of his father's blood on his hands, that the two brothers did not conspire in order that the will not be changed, that a dying man could manage to be so threatening and powerful a creature— all of this I found so difficult to believe even if told under oath, that I am sorry, your Honor, I do apologize humbly, but having a son of my own of this very same age, I was once more overcome."

Mr. Waterman removed his pince-nez, sighed, blew his nose, and turned away from the witness and the judge. With head lowered and step faltering he crossed back to the prosecution table, saying, "Your witness, Mr. Leonard."

# 22

Mr. Leonard called for a short recess before continuing with the testimony. The two of them—lawyer and client—stood at the defense table, consulting earnestly. It was the first chance the spectators had to view Charles close-up, and as the men huddled together, their voices low and incomprehensible to anyone more than a foot away, a constant stream of people wandered up the aisle and paused to stare just outside the enclosure. Once Charles looked over his shoulder at them with a faint look of distaste. A young woman caught the look, gasped, and, red-faced, with a nervous flutter of her hand, grasped the railing. Then, finally confident that she would not faint, she hurried down the aisle to her seat.

The pause in the proceedings gave Emily time to consider the testimony she had just heard. Never before had she given much thought to the manufacture of guns. Her father had a gun and so had Austin, but she had never been able to bring herself to touch either of them. To her, guns had meant the slaughter of animals. She was never able to accept that and had for years refused to eat meat. Yet, incredible as it now seemed, she had not previously thought of guns in relation to the slaughter of people, except during the Civil War. Now, as she considered it, she deemed a country must defend itself, but otherwise could not see justification in the manufacture and keeping of arms.

From where she sat, and especially with the knot of curious spectators behind the barrier, Emily could not see Charles Kidder at all. Yet there was something she felt, that she *discerned*, that banished all others in that room save for Charles and herself. Emily shivered as she considered that, was shocked that she could think such a thing. In this courtroom, he was being painted as the worst sort, a wastrel, a gambler, perhaps a murderer. But Emily sensed in Charles Kidder a power, a glacial determination that was indomitable, rooted and strong. Her heartbeat had quickened as he gave testimony. It seemed to Emily that his impregnability—for even such a force as Mr. Waterman had not shaken him—was kin to her own quiet determination.

She drew back within herself as though wincing at her own thoughts. *She admired Charles Kidder.* Even with the admission, she smiled, for what would Austin or Vinnie or the Farley ladies, or even Otis, think of that? The people of her world thought of her in quite opposite terms. She had always been aware of their attitude but, she realized, had used it to her own best advantage. By allowing those around her to think of her as weak and unable to cope, she had gained immunity from all the nettles of life. She had achieved time and peace to accomplish her own true desires, to write, to be undisturbed in her work. Charles Kidder had followed an opposite path, but his motivations had not been so different.

She leaned back in the seat, unconscious of all the people and the confusion about her, lost in her own thoughts.

She admired Charles Kidder in almost the same way she admired Elizabeth Barrett Browning, curious though it was to link two such disparate people. Yet they shared a strength that had enabled them to break away from domineering fathers and from homes destructively possessive. That same strength had enabled Emily to live an independent and private life, though she remained at home.

At first Emily had come to the courtroom out of her own need to know more about Otis Lord, to see him in his professional role. But her curiosity about Otis had been quickly satisfied and now she was riveted to her seat by the tesimony of the Kidder brothers. All her own confusions, her suppressed hostilities, her private speculations seemed torn from her, exposed. For the first time in her life she had been brought to face all the hidden aspects of herself, and she knew that unless she did, she would never be able to live outside the protection of Amherst.

Attending the Kidder trial had become, in Emily's own life, the most important event since her father's death. And it was her father, and her feelings for him— the love, the fear, the hate—that the trial had made her see. It was as if Emily and her emotions were standing trial along with the Kidders.

The judge's gavel sounded and the spectators rushed to their seats.

"Is your client ready to resume his testimony?" the judge asked.

"He is, your Honor," Mr. Leonard replied.

"Then have him take the stand."

Charles Kidder walked to the witness chair with such sureness, such arrogance, with his finely molded yet obstinate chin so high, that one thought of a parading soldier in full dress.

"The witness remains on oath," the judge reminded the court. "You may proceed, Mr. Leonard."

"Mr. Kidder," Mr. Leonard began in the gravest of tones, "would you tell the court the same story you just told me during the recess his Honor was kind enough to grant?"

"It was the story I wanted to relate when I first took the stand, because I believe it gives a great insight into my father's reflexes, and that my father's reflexes have a great bearing upon this case."

"What exactly do you mean by reflexes?"

"By reflexes I mean the power or lack of power exerted in a moment of severe crisis. And in my father's case, I refer to a *self-inflicted* crisis."

"How old were you when this crisis in your father's life occurred?"

"Ten."

"That would put it at one year after your mother's death, then. Is that correct?"

"It is."

"Objection, your Honor," Mr. Waterman said disdainfully. "If it please the court, I see no relevance in an incident that occurred when the defendant was ten years of age."

"The defendant is on trial for patricide, Mr. Waterman," the judge told him sternly. "Therefore, if the incident in question involves the relationship of father and son, I would deem it relevant to this court and to the case. Proceed, Mr. Leonard."

"I assure the court the incident referred to is highly relevant, your Honor. Mr. Kidder, would you reconstruct that incident to the best of your ability and memory?"

"It was the summer following my mother's death, and Father had taken a cottage by the river. There were several other cottages close by on the shore and Dwight and I had made friends with some boys our own age. We were delirious with happiness. The period since our mother's death had been extremely painful; our house had become a depressing place and it had been an unusually long winter and a very wet spring. But the summer was spectacular and the cottage a cheerful place. Father was in town a lot and we had an immigrant Irish girl to care for us. She had fallen in love with a caretaker nearby, so we were on our own much of the time. Nothing could have pleased us more.

"The day of the incident I wish to relate, we were swimming in the river and the neighbor boys had joined us. As happens with boys that age, there was a good deal of joking about. And much daring. Someone said we wouldn't dare go swimming with no clothes on, and of course, it was only moments before we had stripped off all our clothes and jumped in. We were in such high spirits that we did not hear the approach of my father's carriage. However, our servant girl had, and had come out to the shore to call us. What happened next was somehow so appalling that it seemed a nightmare, and Father was like some monster spawned from one.

"We headed for the shore, and of course, when the water grew shallow, we were exposed. The servant girl let out a cry. Father, who was standing behind her, pushed her aside and turned her away. Then he advanced to the water to meet us. He was shouting curses at us and waving his arms and I remember still the feeling of terror he invoked in me. All of us boys, though, obviously shared the same horror at the sight of his blazing fury, and rather than come out of the water, we drew farther back and went deeper.

"So intensely angry was Father at the offense of our exposure in a public place, he dived right into the water after us, with all his clothes on, and began thrashing wildly in our direction. His power astounded me. None of us were a match for him. He gained rapidly on us and soon was to us. We did not know what to expect. There were five boys and we huddled rather pitifully together. Then, there he was among us, screaming at us that the Devil would take us all, and all the time we were certain that the Devil had already seized him. He went to grab the hair of one boy and the boy bit him. Father beat him in the face and then did get hold of the boy's hair and forcibly pushed him underwater. The other two boys began to cry and to swim away to shore. But something told me that Dwight and I had better get that boy loose or Father would drown him.

"Dwight pulled the best he could at Father's arms to loosen his grasp, but he was helpless against such strength. There was a stick floating in the water and I grabbed it and began to pummel his head as hard as I could. Finally he let go of the boy and fell back and began to thrash around for me. There was blood everywhere and I saw that I had caused a gash in the side of his forehead. He almost had me when Dwight's screams finally penetrated. He had been yelling, 'He didn't come up! He didn't come up!'

"Both Father and I forgot each other in that moment and turned to Dwight. He was treading water next to where the boy had been—and he was alone. The boy had drowned."

"Father then dived under and brought up the boy's body. He swam with it to shore and covered it immediately. The other boys were hiding in the bushes. They had been so frantic in their escape that they had not seen the final moments of the drowning.

"We dressed straightaway and the servant girl went for her friend the caretaker, who knew the boy's family

—they were caretakers of another house on the river—
and then, together, they fetched them and brought them
back. By then we were dressed, the other boys gone, and
Father had his story. He faced the bereaved parents with
great equanimity and told them that all the boys had
been joking about and that their son had obviously had
a cramp in his leg and screamed, but the other boys
thought he was still joking. When they discovered the
truth they shouted for help. He had come, jumped in,
but it had been too late. The boy had drowned. He ex-
plained that he had hurt his head when a stick, propelled
by the sudden current of water stirred up by all the
action, struck him. The grief-stricken parents believed
him. They were, after all, poor, uneducated people.
They thanked him and apologized for all his trouble
when their child had been so foolish. And then they took
their dead child home."

"What did your father say to you about this terrible
sequence of events?"

"He told us he had done God's will and that the boy
had gotten his just punishment, as would we if we ever
spoke about it again or ever exposed our bodies in public.
We returned that very afternoon to town. He fired the
servant girl without notice for her laxity in our supervi-
sion, and as far as my father was concerned, that was the
end of the issue."

"Was it in reality the end?"

"Not for me. I never could forget, nor do I ever
want to do so. It is always in my head as a reminder of
how bestial man can get."

"Was it in your mind the night of June seventh?"

"Vividly."

"Vividly?"

"Yes."

"What brought it so vividly to your mind?"

"There was in my father's face that day the same whipping up of inner devils. He was tortured and furious, with a kind of fury that surpasses human conception."

"When did you note this?"

"When he aimed the gun at me. That was why I was so certain he could shoot me as he had drowned that boy —in monstrous fury."

"Were you and Dwight speaking about the drowned boy when Dwight told you your father had been having terrible nightmares, and you replied that he must be feeling like a murderer, and further stated that you were thankful he would suffer for his deed?"

"Yes, we were."

"Why do you believe your father refused to let Dwight leave home and was so frightened to be alone?"

"I would like to think it was guilt. That he was at least capable of that."

"Do you still maintain that you did not shoot your father?"

"I do."

"And do you maintain that you were not witness to the fatal shot?"

"I heard it but did not see it. And I maintain also that my father was not the helpless man that Mr. Waterman would like to have the court believe. My father was subject to a temper that surpassed his own strength and overcame human frailty. He was a true threat to my survival the night of his death, and a true threat to my brother Dwight's survival. He was also irrational, quite out of his head, and capable of the same bestial behavior I had seen him display in my youth. That behavior had caused a boy's death years before. It easily could have caused Dwight's or my death that night. Dwight was as aware of this as I was."

"Did he speak to you about it?"

"We are identical twins. There are times when words are not necessary between us."

"Thank you very much, Mr. Kidder."

"Is the defense dismissing Mr. Kidder from further testimony?" the judge inquired.

"Yes, your Honor, we are."

"Then you may step down, Mr. Kidder," the judge said, "unless Mr. Waterman would like to cross-examine?"

"No, your Honor," Mr. Waterman said.

Charles Kidder rose instantly, straight and vaguely smiling. He nodded his head as though bowing to the court, and without lagging at all, crossed to his brother's side, where he appeared to salute his brother before seating himself beside him. His attitude conveyed a sense of bravado, a touch of the comic-opera. It was meant apparently to transfer some courage, some perspective to Dwight. But Dwight merely fixed his glance imploringly on his brother's face and sat in petrified silence, like a caught bird shivering even under a hand meant to be gentle.

# 23

*O*tis called for Emily at the Murrays' to take her to the Messassoit Hotel for supper. Not until they were in the carriage and almost there, did Emily ask if they could stop by the Kidder house.

There were lights in the lower windows, like the eyes of crouching wolves. Emily was at first surprised that the house was occupied, then recalled that Maud Hagarty would not have had anywhere else to go.

Long yellow shadows from the lighted windows were strangled and lost in the blackness that surrounded the house. There were no streetlamps and the nearest house was too distant to cast any light. It had been a gusty day, but the wind had died and only a faint rustling of leaves could be heard. Then, from the square in town, came the clamor of bells. It was eight o'clock, about two hours later in the day than when the murder had taken place. At that time, that night, the crime had been committed. Albert Kidder's body had lain sprawled on his bedroom floor, covered by a sheet, waiting to be cut open and inspected like a frog in a classroom laboratory. Emily shivered.

"Do you feel a chill?" Otis asked solicitously.

"No, I was just thinking about the night of the murder."

"I should not have allowed this. We must leave here at once." He leaned forward to tap for the driver, but she drew his hand gently away.

"Not yet," she whispered.

He relaxed beside her and allowed his eyes to grow accustomed to the dark. She had not worn black today, but a curious dress of dark calico which he realized she must have borrowed from the Murray governess. She also wore a crimson-velvet hooded cloak which he recalled seeing Chloe wear to the opera, and which nearly swallowed up the more diminutive Emily. But in the darkness of the carriage, the red appeared more black than her widow's outfit and the expression on her face was lost in its shadows. Her hand, however, was lightly touching his, and he grasped it, holding it tightly so that he could assure himself of Emily's nearness and of the reality of the moment.

"In some book," she said softly, as if confiding a secret of her own, "I read that it was possible that Brutus had been Caesar's son, and I was thinking about that this afternoon. One wonders about the repetition of moments. One wonders what Albert Kidder's last thought was. Perhaps it was something like *"And you, too, Dwight."*

He did not comment, and they sat silently for a time until she began to speak again. "Yes, the repetition of moments. I think about that quite often. How imitative we all are. Not at all singular or unique as our egos would care to have us believe. No! We echo, and ape, and pose, and parody each other, and in a way the past can never die nor the dead remain buried, because we, the living, remain to reproduce all that went before us—evil as well as good, I fear!"

She removed her hand from his and buried it

beneath the fold of the cloak. "Could you understand if I told you that I admire Charles Kidder and that I feel a kinship—a repetition of moments—between both the Kidder brothers and myself?" she asked.

He was glad his surprise was masked by the darkness. It was moment before he allowed himself to reply. "I cannot discuss the Kidder case with you, Emily," he said, "but I understand how, because of the strength of the father, you might identify with it."

Emily desperately wanted to confess, to share with Otis the true impact the Kidder trial had on her. But a lifetime of concealing her emotions made it impossible for her now, though the weight of the situation had become almost too heavy for her to bear alone.

She tried to define Otis' features through the dark in which they sat. She thought that if their eyes could meet in one perceptive glance, she might find the courage to tell him of her feelings of guilt, of why the trial of the Kidders was her trial too. Yet even if she had the courage, the judge could not discuss the case.aThe wind rose again and a branch scraped the top of the carriage.

"Ready?" Otis finally asked, with a measure of impatience.

Emily moved closer to him in the darkness.

"The Messassoit," he ordered the driver, and retrieved her hand.

Otis watched Emily with apprehension as they entered the secluded side entrance of the hotel. A clerk turned his head discreetly away but otherwise no one had seen them arrive. Emily seemed unconcerned. Otis took her arm and they mounted the private staircase together, he not daring to risk speech.

He paused at the door. "If you prefer, we could dine below," he suggested half-heartedly.

"No, I couldn't possibly face all those strangers," she replied.

She stood in the center of the parlor, the crimson hood of her cloak no longer hiding her face. There was about her a very serene and contented air. In the soft light of the fire she looked incredibly young and lovely. All Otis Lord's anxieties fell away, all the love he had ever felt for her seemed to rise in him. And as he saw the trust and the emotion in her face, he thought, *She loves me!* For a moment he was overwhelmed, and he went quickly to her, taking her hands in his.

"My darling Salem," she whispered before he had a chance to speak.

And then they were in each other's arms not holding each other as recent lovers might, but rather as lovers reunited after a very long separation. She had tears in her eyes when they finally drew apart.

For Otis it seemed as though Emily had just come to life, as if he were seeing her truly for the very first time, and when she smiled, looking girlish, her face flushed and reflecting the crimson of her cloak, he thought about their walks in the squire's apple orchard, could see her hair ruffled by a soft westerly wind.

"I wonder as I stand here," she said, her voice now softly resonant, "what you are thinking. For I love you, and I think I must know all there is to know about you. At the same time, because there are apartments in my mind which I believe no one should enter without permission, should I not then respect the seals of others?"

He regarded her fondly. "Yes, seals must be respected," he answered indulgently. "There is always some mystery to love."

"And some mystery in *why* we love *whom* we love?"

"Yes, that as well."

"I know well all the reasons I love you. The mystery, the *wonder*, is your love for me," she said softly, a small tremor in her voice.

He wanted to take her in his arms again, but instinct held him back. "Emily," he said quietly and simply, "I love you for a hundred reasons and for no reason at all. I love you for what you are and I love you for what you may be. There is an aura about you, a presence. It comes from within, elusive probably even to you. I love *that* Emily, too." He smiled wryly. "You might say, Miss Dickinson, that I love you in all your aspects."

She turned away, but only slightly, only to avoid looking at him for a moment. Her cloak fell to the floor with the movement and he retrieved it as she stepped aside and to the fire, gazing into its depths.

"One always hides from oneself, but certain things one knows." She held her chin high and the flame's reflection danced on her throat. "I am only a small brown bird. A sparrow, no more. Contemplating that, your love fills me with awe. But then, then—I have seen a sparrow soar, and that filled me with awe, too. So plain a creature, the color of earth, such drab plummage, and yet, it soared so high it penetrated the deepest blue and passed by many clouds. Grounded, it was a brown sparrow once again, and my awe was transferred to nature's perversity." She faced him now. He had slipped her cloak over the back of a chair and was standing by its side. "Will you love me, darling Salem, when I return to earth?"

"I would if that were true. But you are no sparrow, Emily. You never were. And if you do not see that, then you have truly deluded yourself." He smiled and approached her slowly. His voice was filled with tenderness. "But your true beauty has never eluded me," he said gently. Then, to lighten the atmosphere, he moved to the sideboard, poured them each a sherry and brought the glasses to the fireside, where Emily waited.

"I have ordered dinner," he said. "Shall I have it sent up?"

She raised her face to him and tiny lines of amusement crinkled it. "Perhaps we could sup on love," she suggested, "for if we wait, it may melt like ice cream." As he laughed, her expression became very serious and she put the sherry glass down on a nearby table and clasped her hands tightly together as she looked at him. "Understand, *please* understand, there have been so many sentences I began and never finished, so many small wells I dug and did not fill—"

"Emily, both of us must put away the past," he said gravely. "It is never what it was, but rather what we thought it to be. In most ways you will be a new Emily and I will be a new Otis. Our love will do that for us if each of us endows it with our strength." He was looking at her so earnestly that she had to smile.

He came to her then and took her in his arms. "*Such is my love,*" he recited, "*to thee I so belong, that for thy right myself will bear all wrong. . .* Shakespeare," he added and tilted her chin and leaned down and kissed her gently on the lips. With some surprise he felt a smile blossom there and he drew away, a quizzical look on his face.

"*There are two Mays,*" she recited, "*And a Must, and after that a Shall. How infinite the compromise, that indicates, I will!* Dickinson," she added.

And they both laughed as they walked to the settee, their arms about each other.

*I groped for him before I knew*
*With solemn nameless need*
*All other bounty sudden chaff*
*For this foreshadowed Food*

*Which others taste and spurn and sneer—*
*Though I within suppose*
*That consecrated it could be*
*The only Food that grows*

*E*mily was standing by the window, and on this side of the house, the moon was blocked and there was nothing but the formless darkness beyond. She had not turned on the light, for she had a stronger sense of solitude and privacy in the dark, no longer fearing it, feeling somehow a part of it. She could hear the wind rising and the trees being buffeted. The fire had died down and a chill crept through the room, but Emily hardly felt it as she stared blindly out into the night.

Her thoughts were too difficult to order. They were sharp, jolting flashes, like currents of electricity, and could not be kept alight long enough to identify. Her lips still remembered his lips, her arms his touch, her hand *his*, yet something had slipped away and she could not reconstruct the entire man, the complete feeling.

He had said that one did not remember the past as it truly was, and during the evening, with the present so warm and he so near, she had not thought of the past at all. But here, alone, patches of it were returning. Perhaps it wasn't as she thought it was, but then, she felt compelled to reconstruct it, to rediscover whatever bones of truth were buried there.

*Boston* . . .

She was staying with her two cousins, Loo and Fanny Norcross, not much older than herself, unmarried and recently left parentless. And she was seeing Dr. Williams, the opthalmologist, daily for treatment. It was spring, 1865. She was thirty-five. It seemed that life was over. Her poems had been rejected for publication, now her sight was failing, and she could never declare herself to the man she loved. It was a spring of unseasonable rain, of heat and mosquitoes, and she was feeling like the Prisoner of Chillon, thinking she might never taste freedom again.

Otis had been elected to the Supreme Court that same spring and had come to sit on the bench in Boston; he came alone, Elizabeth being unwell and with no desire to travel.

The first day he called, Emily was sitting by the garden window listening to the sound of the rain. She heard his footstep and turned, knowing it would be him.

"Emily," he said, "poor child." He was by her side, his sleeve damp against her arm. "I heard you were in Boston this very morning, and I haven't been able to think of anything else since. Emily, Emily—I've brought you Shakespeare . . ." His voice broke and he put his hand tenderly on her cheek. "Fate moves in mysterious ways."

He read to her for an hour. Loo served them tea, then left them alone. The rain never stopped, and because with her weakened eyes she saw only the dimmest outline, because the world was wrapped in heavy mist for her—she did not see the night approach.

He came back the next day and the next. He took her for walks in the garden and in the park. Loo and

Fanny thought him kindness itself, a family friend expressing his loyalty.

She had been a new Emily *then*, and he had been a new Otis. And yes, it had been their love that made them so. She had seen the world through his eyes and he had listened to it through her ears.

Summer came and then the fall and then bitter November. That last day she sat once more before the garden window. The first snow had fallen and the whiteness pained her eyes and made them tear.

"Dr. Williams says it will take time, but they are healing," she assured him.

He drew the curtains enough to shield her from any glare. "Those aren't true tears, are they, Emily?"

"I am afraid they might be. Oh, Otis, Otis . . ."

She had run to him and grasped his arm. "Master," she had cried, "I call you that because whatever is dear, whatever is worthwhile, you have taught me."

"Emily dear, you are taking this parting too much to heart," he said soothingly.

"If you saw a bullet hit a bird and he told you he wasn't shot—you might weep at his courtesy, but you would certainly doubt his word!"

"Yes, dear, it wounds me too. But you must return to Amherst."

"Why, *why?*"

"Emily, I haven't the courage for you to remain," he had said in a shaking voice. "Elizabeth will be here for Thanksgiving."

Her arms went limp to her side.

"Please, dear, please forgive me," he begged.

She had gripped the back of a chair to keep from falling. "God made me, Master," she said, fighting back the tears, straining to control her passion. "I didn't just be. I don't know how it was done. He built the heart in me. Bye and bye it outgrew me, and like the little mother —with the big child—I got tired of holding him . . ." She turned to him then. Even in the dim light, even with her weak eyes, she could see the pain on his face. "I gave my heart to you to hold awhile. Are you saying you are giving it back—that the time has elapsed—that you can no longer bear its weight?"

"God forgive me for having to return it, Emily, for surely what we have felt for each other is God's design. But there is no other way. I have weighed it carefully. There is simply *no other way*. Not now. Not in the present. Nor can I ask you to do anything but forget all that has transpired in these months except that a dear friend stood by you when you were ill."

"Don't you understand? You have altered me. I am not the same." She had to clutch the chairback for support. "Have you a heart, sir?" she cried. "Is it set like mine—a little to the left—" She was unable to continue.

"I have been terribly at fault, Emily. I never—" He turned away.

She did not look up as he passed her, and when she did, he was at the door. They exchanged no final words.

She had vowed that moment that she would wait till her hair was gray, if need be; until he carried a cane, for she knew she wanted to see him again, be held by him, loved by him, more than she wanted anything in the world.

She would never know how she regained her composure, how she had held her life so tight that neither Loo nor Fanny had observed her agony when they joined her in the parlor only moments later.

Emily took a few turns up and down the room in the Murray house before sitting on the edge of the bed. She had this terrible premonition, an overwhelming and awesome fear. Shore was within their grasp. Could it somehow be slipping away once again?

She got up quickly, ran to the window, opened it wide, and breathed deeply. The cold air stabbed at her lungs. An iciness ran over her body and she shut the window tight, standing there, hugging herself against the chill that pervaded her being. A light seemed to be dying within her, and with it his face had dimmed, was fading away.

"No, no!" she cried aloud. "I could not stand it. No Lord, no Master . . ."

She fought back the tears and tried to staunch the terror in her heart, this small scared heart with a love too big to contain. She went back to the bed and crawled beneath the covers. She was shivering with a cold so deep within her that it would not dissolve.

It seemed she had slept only long enough to dream a terrible dream, but night had nearly passed. She thought she heard a faint groaning in the attic above, and rose from the bed. There was a far-off quivering thunder in the air. She tied her wrapper close about her and cautiously opened the door to the hallway. The house was silent. Suddenly she thought she heard sounds, achingly close, perhaps from the children's playroom. She tiptoed over to the door that led to that room and gently unlocked it and pushed it open.

There was no window light and it was black inside. There was a candle beside her bed, put there in case a storm should cut off the electricity and she fetched it and lighted it and returned to the playroom. The floorboards creaked and there was the scent of dampness in the air. She went deep into the heart of the room, her own heart beating frantically. She swung around so that the candle would light all the corners. The room was empty. Only the children's lifeless puppets stared open-eyed at her from their wall pegs. She returned immediately to her room and lit a fire, standing so close to it, her face felt aflame.

Then—the night was shattered by the dawn. It took her quite by surprise. Gone were all the groaning sounds, the ghosts, the faded grays. And in the dawn's awakening she clearly saw *his* face, and it was well loved, and well remembered, and it looked at her with living and adoring eyes.

> *"Go tell it"–What a Message–*
> *To whom–is specified–*
> *Not murmur–not endearment–*
> *But simply–we–obeyed–*
> *Obeyed–a Lure–a Longing?*
> *Oh Nature–none of this–*
> *To Law–said sweet Thermopylae*
> *I give my dying Kiss–*

# 25

$\mathcal{L}$ike many men with facile minds but timid souls, Dwight Kidder would have a quick insight into others, and then, like a horse suddenly without blinders, backstep in terror. From the moment he had taken the stand he had known what Mr. Waterman was attempting to do. And then, in a sort of sick fascination, he had realized he was allowing it to happen. The prosecution's aim was to prove that not only was he guilty of murder, but that he was guilty of *premeditated* murder and that Charles was guilty along with him, as it was Charles who had conceived the idea and prodded him into it.

Dwight fixed his gaze on Charles, who glanced back at him with an encouraging smile. It had always been that way. As far back as Dwight could remember, Charles had seemed to have bravado and courage for the both of them, but Dwight knew that with Charles it was more bravado than courage, that only his brother's outward veneer made them appear so disparate.

Both of them shared the dislike for the old house on Carew Street where they had been born. The house was narrow and confined, dark and stuffy and old-fashioned. Both loathed its gloomy walls, its crowded rooms, its smell of dust and decay. Oh, Maud Hagarty had done all she could to keep it clean, but dying things become dust. That was an implacable fact. Sweeping in dark corners could not stop the process. And since their mother's death, the house had died, brick by brick, plank by plank.

Charles had looked away, and Dwight cast his eyes down, as if to look into himself. It seemed important that he order all his thoughts, because in a moment Mr. Waterman and the judge would settle the small argument they were having on a legal point, and Mr. Waterman would turn on him with another barrage of questions.

Dwight felt that he, more than Charles, must be like their mother, though his memory of her was somewhat vague. Still, he recalled her quiet demeanor, her slow smile, her thoughtful expression. She was a dreamer, and so expert a weaver of dreams was she that she lived comfortably under their mystical shelter, seeming, therefore, never to be a part of the reality that existed around her. He understood now how she had been able to come to live in that house and to share it with their father. She never truly *was* there. That was the point. And perhaps that was what Charles never understood. He, Dwight, was never there either.

He felt no greater love for his father than did Charles, nor was his sense of duty stronger, but the fabric of his dreams could not have survived in the world Charles had selected, and he seemed incapable of trading what he had for the unknown. Those dreams still safeguarded him to some extent, otherwise, in view of the terrible events of the last year, he was sure he would have been delivered to madness.

He supposed the world might consider a man who survived on dreams unmanly, but were ambitions anything but dreams? And what was a man without ambition? And wasn't patience a double virtue when coupled with ambition? And did not all successful men have to serve an apprenticeship? The years spent caring for his father were meant to be just that. The doctors' prognosis after his father's first attack had been that he could not possibly live more than five or six years. Then the house and the business interests would be his. No matter how it was stated in his father's will, he would have given Charles his fair share, then he would have sold everything else and bought a boat and sailed the world. He would be a poet and an adventurer and he would live on a floating home that carried him to new and wonderful places. He wondered sometimes what dream had sustained his mother, and at others, felt convinced that some transcendent force had given him his mother's dream.

Well, *they* thought of him as cowardly, weak, susceptible to manipulation by others. Mr. Waterman had been making a very strong point of that, diminishing him to make the case against Charles, which in the end would mean, if the jury believed him, that both of them would be found guilty. Mr. Waterman seemed to have a private enmity toward Charles, almost as though he felt he was a personal threat.

Once more Dwight looked up and over to the dock. Charles had had his gaze set on Mr. Waterman, but something instinctive made him turn toward his brother. He smiled again and nodded his head, as though to say *It will be all right*—then his expression sobered.

Mr. Waterman cleared his throat. "Now, Mr. Kidder, you are twenty-four years of age, are you not? Have you ever thought of marrying?"

Dwight's face changed, colored. The question seemed to take him off guard. "Never seriously," he said.

"What exactly does that mean?"

"Most men my age think about it, I guess, but there was never *anyone* . . ."

"Had you not had the responsibility to care for your father, would you not have considered marriage seriously?" Mr. Waterman prodded.

Mr. Leonard rose to his feet. "Objection—"

"Is this line of questioning truly pertinent, Mr. Waterman?" Judge Lord interrupted.

"With due respect, your Honor, I believe it is," Mr. Waterman said.

"I believe counsel is invoking innuendo, your Honor, and I object strenuously."

Judge Lord considered the situation for a moment or two, and then quietly, as though thinking aloud, concurred with the defense. "Objection sustained," he said.

Mr. Waterman shifted his weight in irritation, walked a few steps away from the witness, and then turned to face him. "Did you know your brother was arriving home on the seventh of June last, Mr. Kidder?" he asked, his voice now abrasive.

"I thought it possible."

"Had you been in communication?"

"Yes."

"Had he written you that he planned to come on that day?"

"He had."

"Then why had you not informed Miss Hagarty? Why did you allow her to prepare trays for two for supper when you knew there would be three?"

"I did not know that for sure. Charles was in New York that week. He wrote only that he would try to come up on the seventh."

"But why on the seventh especially, Mr. Kidder?"

"It was the day that he expected to conclude his business in New York."

"And I put it to you, Mr. Kidder, that it was also the one day of the month that Miss Hagarty could be relied upon to be away from the house. Further, you *insisted* that she be out of the house on her off day, even though her desires were otherwise. Is that not the way it was, Mr. Kidder?"

"No!" Dwight cried out and glanced desperately over to Charles.

As he did so, Mr. Waterman stepped sideways and blocked the dock from the witness' view. "Had your brother told you that if he came he would arrive on the five-fifteen?" he persisted.

"It is the only train on that day from New York."

"And what time was Miss Hagarty expected to return?"

"She was not required to return until eight or nine. A reasonable hour. She actually did not have to help in the house until seven the next morning. But she was— *is*—like a member of the family. She, therefore, did not regard those allowances as mandatory."

"Therefore, you could, I assume, expect her home earlier than eight or nine in the evening, is that correct?"

"Yes."

"How early?"

"Six."

"Was that purely speculation, Mr. Kidder, or had you *insisted* she *not* return before six that evening?"

"I had told her she certainly would not be needed before that time."

"And you did not inform her your brother might arrive for supper, even though you knew how fond she was of him and how loyal a girl she was and that if she knew he might have been arriving at that hour, she would have wanted to return early to prepare for his arrival. I ask you why, Mr. Kidder?"

"Because she would have returned early, and out of fairness I believed she was entitled to and should receive a full day off each month."

"Really, Mr. Kidder?" Mr. Waterman took off his pince-nez and stared at the witness in disbelief, as though somehow his glasses had deceived him. "You are quite certain that your sense of fair play was not, instead, a plot, a device to keep Miss Hagarty out of the house until six, giving your brother time to arrive in Springfield, get to the house, and therefore assist you in your evil and *premeditated* plot?"

"Objection!"

"Sustained."

Dwight's lips trembled. There was fear in his eyes and he clenched and unclenched his hands. Mr. Waterman stood obdurately, still blocking Charles from his sight. He glanced desperately around the courtroom, and not able to catch Mr. Leonard's eye, for his was on the judge, settled on a nervous defense assistant, who could do no more than shrug his shoulders in answer to this silent plea.

"All right, Mr. Kidder," Mr. Waterman was saying, "let us put aside Maud Hagarty for the moment." He now moved a few steps so that Dwight could see Charles quite clearly. "Your brother reached the house by five-twenty. I know that because a check of the time schedule for that day shows the New York train was three minutes early, and a further investigation has turned up the cabby who drove your brother from the station to Carew Street." He withdrew a neatly folded slip of paper from his pocket. "This, your Honor, is a sworn statement from the cabdriver, one Rufus Hawkins, of River Street. If I may, I shall enter it as evidence."

"Bailiff," the judge called.

The bailiff stepped up and took the paper and then passed it to the jury.

"In his statement Mr. Hawkins identifies your brother Charles as the man he picked up at the depot from the five-fifteen on the seventh of June. At most, the ride from the station to Carew Street is not more than a five-minute trip. Even so, your brother appeared impatient and very much in a hurry, and was greatly irritated when the driver, obeying the laws, would not go faster. It took, therefore, near enough to the usual five minutes. Your brother handed the driver an amount considerably in excess of the fare and did not wait for change. That would put him in the house near enough to five-twenty to call it so. Now, Mr. Kidder, did you come down and open the door for your brother?"

"No."

"Did he have a key?"

"He did."

"I see. Did he come up to your father's room and greet you there?"

"I heard him enter, and went out into the hallway."

"Did he call out?"

"No."

"Even so, you were sure it was Charles, is that correct?"

"No, but I went out into the hall to investigate."

"And how long did you remain there with your brother?"

"Only a minute or so. Father had recognized his voice and called out for us to come into the room."

"Did you do so?"

"Yes."

"What happened then?"

Dwight shifted his gaze nervously from Charles to Mr. Leonard. The latter slowly nodded his head, as if to say *It is quite all right, tell your story.*

"We both came into the room and close to the bed." Dwight's face grew blank for a moment, as if his thoughts had retreated behind a drawn curtain.

"Yes, Mr. Kidder?" Mr. Waterman urged.

"It had been such a beautiful day. Really summer-like. The sky had been the brightest blue and the sun had poured through my father's window. Now it was gone and it was turning dark, and as I had been resting in the chair by my father's bed, I had not lighted the lamps. There was a fire in the hearth. I had set it about four o'clock when the air began to cool. We kept the room as warm as possible even in summer, due to Father's condition. But the fire was low by then and all of us looked like shadows—undefined, like shadows . . ."

Dwight tried to continue, but could not immediately do so. He lifted a trembling hand to his eyes and wiped it across them as if to remove a veil. The courtroom was still and waiting.

"Are you able to continue, Mr. Kidder?" Judge Lord asked.

Dwight looked up at him with some surprise, as though not expecting to see him there.

"The court is waiting for you to continue, Mr. Kidder," Mr. Waterman said in a jarring voice.

"Yes . . . yes . . . I remember thinking it was all a dream, that it was not real, that my father was not in the room, nor Charles, nor I. And I remember thinking, too, that I must keep the *memory* in my mind. That is, the *sense* of those moments."

"You stood by your father's bed. Continue, please."

"I remember feeling very tired. I had had little sleep the night before, and almost immediately Father began an argument with Charles. I could feel real pain in my head, I was so tired."

"What were they arguing about?"

"Father's will. He had been prodding me about it all week. It was one of the reasons I had written Charles he should come home—to settle the business of the will—because until he did so, I was certain my father would remain in a terrible state."

"What disturbed your father about his will?"

"He had cut Charles out of it."

"Everything was then to go to you?"

"There was a sum to go to Maud. One thousand dollars. Otherwise it was all to go to me."

"And he wanted to change that?"

"Yes, he wanted Charles to receive all the monies that came in from some stock he had been given when he sold his business to Smith and Wesson."

"What kind of stock was it?"

"Shares in Smith and Wesson. He knew, of course, Charles's adamant feelings about taking money from the manufacture of arms, and that was all part of it. He seemed to require, for his own peace, that Charles's position be reversed. That is why he did not want him to have a share in the house or in the cash, but all his shares in Smith and Wesson."

"Were they valuable?"

"To my standards. They were worth more than the house, more than any or all of my father's possessions. And they keep increasing in value."

"I take it, then, that he did not mince words and that he came out directly and told your brother this, is that correct?"

"Yes."

"How did your brother react to this information?"

"He was angry and he refused the bequest and told my father that if he did receive them, he would sign the shares away. My father grew very irate and I was afraid he might suffer a stroke. I asked Charles to come down into the kitchen with me to help ready the supper trays. We convinced my father we would be gone only a few minutes and he agreed to let us both go."

"How long were you away from the room?"

"No more than a few minutes, when we heard a terrible crash. We left what we were doing and ran back up to Father's room." He pressed his pale lips together and was silent.

"Where did you find your father when you reached the room?"

Dwight sat quietly for a long moment. Then, as though a door was opening on a distant memory, he continued. "The light was very faint and uncertain. It had a curiously red glow. It all seemed more unreal than it had before."

"Where was your father?" Mr. Waterman repeated.

It took a moment before Dwight could reply. "On the floor," he said in a shaky voice. "He was huddled over and gasping for breath. At first I thought he had another attack, but then I saw the open drawer where he had kept his handgun, and saw what looked like . . . the light was so dim . . . but it looked like a gun in his hand, grasped close to his body. I realized that he was too far away from the bed to have fallen out of it, and that he had had enough strength to get out of the bed, open the drawer, take out the gun, and start to walk toward the door. Then I felt very sick and I thought I might not be able to keep my stomach down. It was so hot in the room, and since Maud had not come in to freshen it, there was the smell of sweat and sickness. It almost overcame me. That, and the terror of the moment."

"Why were you so filled with terror, Mr. Kidder?"

"Because I knew somehow that Father planned to use that gun." He looked down at his tightly clenched hands. "I knew—because he was now sure that Charles *would* sign away his interest in the arms industry, which was his great and driving force—that he would kill

Charles." He glanced up and his eyes held and locked with Mr. Waterman's. It was the first show of any strength that Dwight Kidder had shown since he had taken the stand. "You see, I knew he could kill a man in cold blood. I knew he believed other life was lesser than his and that his will should be done."

The sound of the courtroom clock seemed loud in the room. Many a spectator mopped his brow, and several ladies appeared pale-faced and somewhat queasy, as if they could feel the closeness of Albert Kidder's sickroom and smell the foul odor of the dying.

"Did you go to help your father back to his bed?"

"No . . . no . . ." Dwight Kidder's voice was almost inaudible.

"Speak up, Mr. Kidder," the judge requested.

"No," the witness repeated in a thin but clear voice.

"Why did you not immediately go to assist an infirm man from the floor where he had fallen?" Mr. Waterman asked with heavy condemnation.

"I was no longer sure he was as infirm as he claimed. And I was quite certain, as I said before, that he had a gun and meant to use it."

"Against you?" Mr. Waterman sneered with amazement.

"He was capable of it."

"What did you do then, Mr. Kidder?"

"Father's face was white—not pale from illness but white with rage. I saw him stretch out one hand to support himself, but he held the gun in the other and it was pointed at me. He meant to stop me from leaving with Charles. For a moment I thought he was going to pull the trigger, and I fell to the floor hoping that way to protect myself. Charles commanded his attention then and Father turned the gun toward him and aimed it. I crawled forward and grabbed his leg. It was like it had been that time in the river. There was only my father and a force that was resisting him. He was bound and determined to squash it anyway he could. I was certain of that.

"He was shouting at Charles even as I pulled him down to the floor. We began wrestling for the gun. I could not believe his strength. He was screaming and carrying on like a madman. I knew I had to quiet him or he would have a seizure. I could not understand really why he had not had one already.

"I held his hand, trying to wrest the gun from him. He fought wildly and the butt of it caught him on the side of his head. Incredibly, he was still conscious, and ready to continue the struggle." Real fright, real suffering mingled with Dwight's recitation. He paused, his lips quivering and his shoulders shaking. He lifted his clenched fists to his mouth and bit into his knuckles. A small sob escaped and with it words that were more like a gasp. "Then I shot the gun and saw the blood ooze from his shoulder."

Dwight Kidder was sobbing softly.

Mr. Leonard jumped quickly to his feet. "I beg the court's indulgence," he said, "but the witness seems unable to continue."

"Is that so, Mr. Kidder?" Judge Lord asked.

Dwight Kidder drew himself up, visibly controlling himself.

"Are you able to continue, Mr. Kidder?" Judge Lord inquired.

The witness nodded his head in the affirmative. He wiped his eyes and blew his nose and stuffed the handkerchief back into his pocket. The bailiff brought him water and he drank it slowly. All the time the court sat breathlessly, fearful of making a sound, as though Dwight Kidder were a wild creature who would dart away at any human stirring.

"You shot the gun and wounded your father in the shoulder, is that correct?" Mr. Waterman asked in a dispassionate voice.

The witness agreed with a nod of his head.

"Did you *then* go to aid your father?"

"He *still* managed to get to his knees. I remember hearing Charles say, '*I'll go for Dr. Crane,*' but I never saw him. I had my eyes riveted on my father." He drew a sharp and audible breath. Then he sat up straight. There was a sense of courage about his attitude now that was immediately visible to everyone in the courtroom. "I remembered the blood that had swirled around him when Charles had hit him with a stick to get him to release that drowning boy. It all seemed to be happening again for me. He was saying *Give me the gun, Dwight, give me the gun*—and there was more sureness in his voice than there had been in years. Something in the desperateness of the struggle had brought out a superhuman strength in him. No, an animal quality. He was the lion who had been injured and fought now with a terrible might."

Dwight's voice became quite cool, almost distant. "I knew if I handed him the gun he would have no choice but to shoot me. I shot him instead. The bullet went into his chest. He kneeled there, poised for a second, and I threw the gun from me and it landed in front of him. Then he collapsed on top of it. He didn't even gasp. Not one more sound before he died. And then—it was such a curious thing. The fire died out at the same time and the room seemed filled with shadow and smoke—and *spirit.*"

Dwight Kidder was silent.

Mr. Waterman stood without emotion. He waited a moment and then turned his back on the witness and faced the jury. "You have just heard a very poignant and moving testimony. If we are to interpret it correctly, the witness is presenting a case of self-defense. Self-defense against a man bedridden for nearly five years, a man the dotors called a dying man! Even so, this was a testimony on oath, and an open mind should tend it. But, lady and gentlemen of the jury, I am very much afraid that is an impossibility due to the evidence I have in my hand." At a point before these last words he had taken another folded document from his pocket.

"Is that evidence to be presented to the court?" Judge Lord asked.

"Yes, your Honor. May I read it aloud before passing it in as evidence?"

"You may."

"It is a letter in Dwight Kidder's hand, written on the first day of June, 1881, to his brother Charles, and it was found just two days after the murder by investigating officers in the trash bin of a hotel in New York City where Charles Kidder had been registered. The letter reads as follows:

> *"June 1st. 1881*
>
> *"Charles,*
>
> *"The situation here grows more desperate and calls for immediate action. The seventh is Maud's day off. If you can get here before six we will be assured privacy with Father and our plan. He keeps a gun by his bed. Left-hand side. Remember that. I dare not remove it before, as he will immediately miss it. I am thinking of buying a boat when this is all over and sailing the world. Want to come?"*
>
> *"Dwight"*

The bailiff collected the letter and entered

it as evidence. Mr. Waterman shook his massive head and heaved a heavy sigh.

"Your witness, Mr. Leonard," he said and sat down at his table.

## 26

*T*here was no doubting it, this last piece of evidence had struck a serious blow to the case for the defense. Even Mr. Leonard, whose cool demeanor had become one reliable of the case, appeared noticeably disturbed. From the letter's content, there seemed no other interpretation save that the Kidder twins had conceived a plot to murder their father and had implemented and carried it through. Also, Mr. Waterman's timing had been brilliant. He had held the evidence until Dwight had completed his account of the death of his father, thereby negating the entire testimony, which was meant to mitigate the charge of first-degree murder to manslaughter on the witness' behalf and to exonerate Charles almost entirely.

A five-minute recess was called for by the defense, and granted. Dwight stepped down from the stand, and was immediately surrounded by Mr. Leonard and his assistants. Quite perversely, in the entire courtroom, Dwight Kidder, and he alone, appeared unstirred. A great change had come over him during the last minutes of his testimony. Somehow he had sailed the rough seas.

They were behind him. Whatever else happened in that court, in telling his story, he had released all the built-up storm inside him. With a noose closer about his neck than at any other time in the trial, Dwight Kidder felt giddy, a bit intoxicated. There was even a small but distinct smile curling the edges of his mouth.

Mr. Leonard was very worried and strongly considered not allowing Dwight to return to the stand. That thought was at the back of his mind as he questioned his client hotly about the new evidence.

"Did you write that letter, Dwight?" he asked.

"Yes." Dwight continued smiling.

"What did you mean by a *plan?*" Mr. Leonard whispered, his arm around Dwight's shoulder to turn him away from curious eyes.

"We meant to drug him. I had all those pills the doctor had given me. Then we were going to call Dr. Crane and tell him Father was in a coma and then have him moved in that condition to a private hospital, where he would be committed." Dwight spoke in an offhand manner, as though giving ingredients for a recipe.

A thought immediately flashed into Mr. Leonard's mind. "That pill you gave him, that Charles mentioned in his testimony—"

"There were more than one. That was when we tried to drug him. But we didn't succeed. He refused the pills and would not take any liquids."

"He guessed?"

Dwight nodded his head.

Mr. Leonard released his hold on the young man and turned away. He stood, thoughtful and calculating. His eyes were bright with speculation, and his keen mind passed quickly over and weighed all the alternatives in a matter of minutes. When he turned back to Dwight, his decision had been made. He patted Dwight reassuringly on the shoulder and went over to Charles and spoke briefly to him. Charles looked very concerned, but he nodded his head in apparent agreement. Then Mr. Leonard faced the bench. "Your Honor," he called out.

"Yes, Mr. Leonard?"

"If it please the court, I will forgo questioning of this witness and would instead like to recall Mr. Charles Kidder to the stand."

"It is highly irregular."

"I know, your Honor, but my esteemed colleague has entered a piece of evidence that relates directly to Charles Kidder, and the defense feels that only Charles Kidder can clarify that evidence for the court's true benefit."

Across the room Mr. Waterman held back his exasperated breath. The defense was going to keep Dwight off the stand for obvious reasons. But to put Charles back on—that could mean only one thing. Leonard had something up his sleeve. It riled the attorney general that he could not figure out what it might be.

Charles returned once again to the stand. Mr. Leonard was not the impassive questioner he had been previously. He paced to and fro before the witness for a moment or two, then stopped, and with his hands tightly grasping the rail of the stand, leaned in as close to Charles as he was able and spoke in a very slow, strong, and moving voice.

"Mr. Kidder, I know this will be difficult for you. Believe me, my heart both understands and aches for the revealment I am now asking you to make to aid this court in dealing justly with this case. I want you, I *ask* you, Mr. Kidder, to explain to the court the true meaning of your brother's words in his letter to you—that letter having been entered by the prosecution as evidence." Mr. Leonard straightened and stepped back a few steps. "With the court's indulgence, I trust it will give Mr. Kidder time to explain fully and in his own words, your Honor."

"Granted, Mr. Leonard."

"Please take your time, Mr. Kidder. As I said, I know this is very difficult." Mr. Leonard then stepped aside so that almost everyone in the courtroom, most especially the jury, would have an unblocked view of the witness.

Charles placed his hands out flat on the stand, seeming in one way to be gaining physical support in so doing, but in another to be honest with the court. Whether it was a calculated gesture or not, it worked well on his behalf. In that position it was difficult not to believe everything he was about to say.

"I had not been home in over a year," he began in a clear and straightforward voice, "but Dwight and I corresponded regularly. During my last trip I had seen a decline in my father's condition, but what had concerned me to a much greater extent was Dwight's own decline. He had lost all contact with the outside world. He had no friends, saw no girls, seldom left the house or my father's bedside. I could see a tragic thing taking place. Dwight had sublimated all his natural instincts. He was becoming one of those harridans who haunt hospital corridors and who live on death and the dying. We had words about it. As a witness has stated, we even came to blows.

"This was out of the deepest fraternal concern, believe me. Twins are like a part of each other. I know my brother almost as well as I know myself. Better, perhaps, because we do not always face the truth of ourselves. He was softer than I, but not weaker. No, in the long run it was I who was the weakest. One should not confuse softness with weakness. They have little to do with one another.

"Dwight was soft and sensitive, brighter than I, the

intelligent one, really. There was another country harbored in his mind—he lived there with great immunity for years. But on that last visit I saw that that country was not as impregnable as I had believed.

"I saw these changes in him and I knew he had to be forced somehow away from being a keeper of chamber pots and a taker of temperatures. I wanted to have Father committed to a good hospital where paid nurses would tend his needs. He refused to speak to Father about this, and it was obvious that Father's agreement had to be secured first.

"With the arrival of each new letter I could see that Dwight was growing closer to the end of his tether. I was frantic that he could suffer a physical or mental collapse. I began pressing the case for having Father committed to hospital. Dwight wrote back saying Father would never agree to such a thing. I answered that it then had to be accomplished without Father's agreement.

"Father was being given medication to calm him, for even small irritations seemed to excite him dangerously. I finally convinced Dwight that we could sufficiently drug Father so that he would be in a coma and yet not endanger his life if we got him immediately to hospital. Once in the hospital, we would have to get the doctors to cooperate with us—at least until the time that I could get Dwight out of the house in Carew Street and embarked on a life of his own. That was the plan that Dwight spoke of in his letter to me."

"How did you expect to accomplish this, Mr. Kidder?" Mr. Leonard asked soberly.

"We did not want to involve Maud, so we decided it could only be achieved on her off day. The nearest one, as the letter states, was to be the seventh of June. It was not easy for me to return that day, but I felt I must and that the outcome of our plan must be accomplished then or it would be too late for Dwight.

"All the details of my arrival have been presented to the court, so I shall not repeat them, and all I have stated to this court has been the truth. There was one omission, however,"

"What was that?"

"When Dwight tried to force Father to take the medication, Father refused to swallow the dosage. Somehow he guessed. He grew intensely angry. That was when Dwight and I left him alone and went downstairs. After the shooting I realized he might have thought we meant to kill him. That must have been why he could turn on Dwight with a gun, why he went so wild. But . . ."—his voice rose and his shoulders with it—"at no time did we ever consider murder. As I have repeated to the court over and over again, and as I repeated to my father, I could not bear firearms and have not—nor would I—touch a gun to this day."

"Mr. Kidder," Mr. Leonard said gently, the kindly doctor now, or the concerned neighbor, "would you tell this court what happened after the terrible *accident* of your father's death—"

"Objection!"

"Strike the word *accident*, if you like, your Honor," Mr. Leonard said, making sure the jury heard the word repeated.

"It shall be done, Mr. Leonard. Continue with your questioning of the witness," Judge Lord ordered.

"Would you be kind enough to tell this court the sequence of events directly *after* your father's death, Mr. Kidder?"

"I had started down the stairs for help and for Dr. Crane, when I heard the final bullet. I returned immediately to the room. My father was dead. Dwight stood a few feet from the body. I could not see the gun. And actually, the room had grown so dark that I could just make out Dwight's form. He looked *queer* and for a moment I thought he might have lost his reason. I said, 'Come with me, Dwight, we'll go to Dr. Crane's.' But he did not move. He simply stood there staring into the dead fire.

"There is a back way to the doctor's and I took it. When I got to his house he was leaving it with Maud, whom I had forgotten completely. They did not see me and they were both hurrying in the direction of our house. I did not want to call them back and so delay them, and I assumed that with the doctor on his way, Dwight would be taken care of. Father was dead. There was nothing that could be done for him. But for the first time since the terror of those last few minutes, I recognized that the situation was a grave one and that the police might become involved. I felt Dwight especially needed legal aid and I recalled that you did not live far away. I hastened to your house, Mr. Leonard, from which, as you know, you were absent. But a servant permitted me to wait for your return. You came home about nine-fifteen and I told you the sequence of events, though I did not include the plan to drug Father. At that time neither of us realized that Dwight had followed me out of the back door of our house and was at that time just wandering around the streets of Springfield in a shocked state. I assumed that Dr. Crane had sedated him and that he was safe in the care of Maud, at least for that night."

"Did you leave town?"

"No, I did not. I checked into a hotel under an assumed name and waited. Dwight was picked up and placed in the county jail before morning and charged with Father's murder."

"Would you say your brother was in a state other than normal when you saw him standing over your father's body?"

"He appeared to be in some sort of coma or trance."

"Had he appeared normal earlier?"

"Dwight had not seemed himself for a very long time."

"Thank you, Mr. Kidder, thank you," Mr. Leonard said humbly.

"Your Honor," Mr. Waterman addressed the bench.

"Yes, Mr. Waterman?"

"May I have the right to cross-examine the witness?"

"Proceed."

The two attorneys passed each other as Mr. Waterman started toward the witness and Mr. Leonard returned to the defense table.

"Mr. Kidder, I ask you only one question on the basis of this new testimony. Did you, in league with your brother, Dwight, plot, not to shoot your father dead as the final outcome was, but to overdose him so that he would die quietly and in a coma?"

"Your Honor," Mr. Leonard began.

"We did not!" Charles stated firmly. "The facts are exactly as I have stated."

"Well, I put it to you, Mr. Kidder, that the facts are not all there in your testimony. I put it to you that it was your design to drug your father and leave him to die, so that you and Dwight could then legally claim the estate and so that your father's death would appear accidental. You and your brother conspired in this undertaking and you came to Springfield for this purpose only. Further, Mr. Kidder, when your father realized this and fought for his life, you did nothing whatsoever to stop your brother from completing the act with the aid of a gun. You, Mr. Kidder, who so loudly professed such a profane hatred of firearms, did nothing to stop your brother from pulling a trigger and shooting your father to death. Did nothing, Mr. Kidder, because you hated your father, wanted him dead, and because you would benefit greatly by his death. All this twaddle about changing the will had no relevance whatsoever, because you and your brother were acting as one, and wherever you wanted to believe your share of the money came from, your brother would still make sure you received a fit share and you knew this!"

"Objection!" Mr. Leonard screamed throughout Mr. Waterman's short filibuster. But the attorney general would not be stopped either by the shouts of Mr. Leonard or the judge's gavel until he had said what he had wanted to say, and by that time the damage had been done. Eleven men and one woman riveted an accusing eye at the young man on the witness stand.

The closing pleas on both sides were eloquent and worthy of the counsels. It took the jury longer than the court expected for them to bring in a verdict.

It was *guilty*, on both counts.

Sentencing was set for the next morning. The Kidder twins were returned to their individual cells. They were given dinner. Dwight ate none. A minister came to speak with them. Dwight was silent. In the morning they found Dwight had hanged himself.

With great sadness, Judge Lord passed sentence of twenty years' imprisonment on Charles. It was justice, of course. A jury had declared him guilty, and life had leveled its own justice on the father. Albert Kidder had died by the gun and his arms-manufacturing interests went to the state.

# 27

Otis Lord came to Henry Murray's office to seek advice. He had always trusted Henry's instincts and judgment. The matter of his present deep concern was his career, and Henry had watched that career more closely than any other man Otis knew.

Judge Lord's verdict in the Kidder case had met with contrasting and paradoxical reactions. His popularity with the general public, the extent of admiration from the liberal forces, had always created a bitterness against him among conservatives. But the trial had neatly turned the tides. It was now the liberals who abused him and the conservatives who sang his praises. And the keenness of the hostility in proportion to the warmth of support, and the quarter from which each came, afflicted him with distress.

As soon as the verdict was in and sentence passed, the conservative press rushed to commend his virtues. In all ways they were treating him like a candidate for public office. The liberal press, on the other hand, editorialized against him forthwith. The battle appeared to be on, and though he had been pressured and pursued, he had not accepted a candidacy. He was well aware that if one side trumpeted him as a demi-god, the other side must run him down as a demi-devil. But all his sensibilities had been affronted, for at no time had he considered himself more than a tool of justice.

The minute Otis Lord walked into the office, Henry could see that his friend was greatly disturbed, and his first action was to ask his secretary to close the door and under no circumstance to interrupt them. Then he rose and came around his desk and greeted Otis warmly. "Come, sit down," he commanded pleasantly. "I'll pour us both a brandy."

"You have read the papers, I would suspect," Otis began as soon as he had seated himself in a leather club chair.

"Glanced at them," Henry admitted, and handed his friend a glass. "Cheers."

"I am *not* running for office," Otis declared.

"I didn't think you would." Henry took his drink and went back to sit behind his desk. "The conduct of the press is reprehensible," he said, "but certainly not astonishing. Surely, no matter which way the verdict and sentencing went you must have known you were running your head into the lion's mouth! This has been a sensational case, carried not only in the state, but nationwide, and the coming election is sadly lacking in both issue and candidates."

"I am very heavy in heart, Henry. It rankles me that any man should be exploited, myself most apparently included. But the wound goes deeper."

"How deep?" Henry asked incautiously.

"I am doubting justice as now represented in our courts."

"I take it you do not feel the jury returned a just verdict. Is that it?"

"A jury is composed of people. And they do not rise above their own emotions simply by becoming a jury." His voice was brittle, his face reflected pain.

Henry sat back in his chair, holding his brandy glass, never removing his glance from his friend's troubled face. "What is it you intend to do, Otis?" he asked slowly. "I am not sure but I am considering retiring from the bench," Otis replied, and then, appearing relieved, he breathed deeply before asking, "What would you say to that?"

Henry stirred restlessly in his chair. His hand clenched the brandy glass. "Well, that is not a new consideration," he said directly. "Be honest with yourself, Otis. You have been thinking about this, munching on it for a long time now. Hell, man, you were a damned sight happier in practice. Admit it to yourself and understand why. It is a much more active, a much more vigorous, endeavor. But even more, Otis, pursuing law, you are a doer—sitting on the bench, you become a viewer. That is not your style. Never was. It was contingent to the life that pleased Elizabeth and you found that necessary for your survival."

"I am talking about more than life styles," Otis said.

"All right," Henry continued. "You were concerned about the carriage of justice in this case and so you are doubting the process of law. Shall I tell you how many times I have done the same thing? No, I shall not bore you. It would be an endless recitation."

Otis sat quietly, his hands cupped around the brandy glass. Whatever he wanted to say did not come easy to him, but Henry waited patiently.

"I think I *must* step down from the bench, Henry," he finally confessed. "I do not believe my heart can stand the weight or the strain any longer."

Henry put down his glass and glanced meaningfully

around his office. It was the workroom of a successful lawyer; framed diplomas on the paneled walls, mahogany desk, leather furniture, row on row of bound books. "You will, of course, go back into practice," he said evenly.

"I . . . I don't know."

Henry's fist hit the desk. "You don't know!" he shouted. "Are you proposing retirement? Otis, you know that would be a damned-fool way to spend the rest of your years! Be sensible. Be honest. Come back to law. Join me in my firm. I have offered you a partnership before. I will offer it to you right now. You could be happy and vital and fulfilled here, and Miss Dickinson would be happy in Springfield. She has friends. There are cultural elements in the city."

Otis smiled. Henry's words pleased him because he knew how deep-felt they were. "Thank you, Henry," he said. "I will consider it."

Henry carefully selected a cigar from his humidor and lighted it. "Be damned sure you really do, Otis," he finally said.

"Oh, I will be damned sure." He laughed lightly. Then they were quiet again and Otis retreated to a private area of his mind while Henry puffed happily on his Havana.

"What do you think of Emily?" Otis asked at last.

Henry considered the question very seriously before replying. "She is a very exceptional lady," he said carefully. "Full of wonder and pain. The price one must pay for being exceptional, I suppose." He tapped the tip of his cigar on a crystal ashtray. "She is a dreamer and there is another life she lives in her imagination. I believe in the integrity of both. But she has that—*integrity.* More, a kind of intensity. Like her? I am not sure anyone having met Emily Dickinson could settle for such a simple judgment. I am struck by the tenseness she exudes, fascinated at her counterclockwise manner of living. I mean, she *does* go against the order of things—and I find her as a woman more appealing with each encounter, though I am not sure I would want to be married to her. No offense intended!" He got up and came around the desk again, facing his friend, leaning casually against the front of the desk to bring him closer to eye level with Otis.

"You have yourself a bit of mystic territory there, Otis." He smiled gently. "It will not be easy, but living with a woman never is."

"Nor living without one," Otis added.

Both men laughed, and then Otis left and returned to the Messassoit to pack.

Emily, calmly and without hurrying, returned the few things that she had brought with her to Springfield back into her small suitcase. She was not anxious to leave. She had become quite fond of the chestnut tree beneath her window, of the circular window itself, of the sound of the children playing on the lawns outside, and of the deep-throated bark of Clipper as he chased them. In the week she had been at the Murrays' the leaves had come out on the trees and were now green and spreading. They would, of course, be the same at home, but she did not want to think about home just yet.

Somehow she was pleased that she was dressed in mourning. She had been truly overcome when she had been told about Dwight Kidder's suicide and saddened by the thought of Charles Kidder spending the best years of his life in prison. There was much to mourn! Her dress was very much in order. Still, she had not been as distraught as all the members of the Murray household seemed prepared for her to be. She now had some other strength to lean upon which protected her from such excesses.

She would leave very early the next morning and Sue was to go with her, but that was still a distant prospect. She would spend the evening with Salem. He would, in fact, be around in a carriage in an hour's time to fetch her.

A slightly ironic smile spread across her face. The scales of justice were about to balance. The storms and distresses were behind her. She was about to sail into a snug harbor. She stood in front of the porthole window, but the greens fused and the late-day sun distorted and misted the view. Instead, she could see only Salem's face. He was gray and taciturn and there was a suggestion of pouches beneath his eyes. And those eyes were as deep a blue as the sky on this clear spring afternoon, and his large ruddy face as vital as the wind that was now rising. And at the root of the wind was the spark that ignited life.

They came and called her for tea. It was served in the dining room, and the children and Chloe and Shauna DePeters were present. It was a very festive occasion and had the feeling of a child's birthday party. Emily was touched because she knew she was the honored guest. The room was warm and Chloe's plump, still-smooth face was flushed as she fanned herself with a lace-edged cambric handkerchief.

"Isaiah, do close your mouth when you are eating," she was saying. "Deborah, take your elbows off the table." She turned to Emily and her voice was good-humored, pleasant. "You shan't miss all this clatter, I am sure."

"But I shall," Emily replied.

A look of pleasure passed over Chloe's kindly face. Isaiah got off his chair and began to clap his hands and jump about and shout. "The present! The present!" he chirped.

"Isaiah!" Chloe reprimanded. "Stop jumping about and carrying on and shouting like an Indian!" She was immediately aware of Miss DePeters seated across from her. "I am sorry, dear, that is just an expression. It was not meant—"

"Please, there is no need to apologize," Miss DePeters quickly said. She rose, and taking Isaiah's hand, started out of the room. "Please excuse us for a moment."

They returned with a large package tied with bright scarlet ribbons and placed it before Emily.

"Oh, do be careful with the ribbons," Jerusha whispered into Emily's ear.

"Would you like them for your hair?" Emily asked.

"Oh, please, yes, thank you!" Jerusha blushed.

The box contained three little hand puppets the children had made, each in his own likeness. They were crude and amusing and hurriedly put together, but Emily had never been so touched by a gift before. She thought she might cry from happiness. She looked around the table at Chloe and her children and her heart brimmed over.

The carriage arrived shortly thereafter. Emily ran to greet it as though she were one of Chloe's brood. The wind had risen and it was crisp and splendid and swept her along. Otis jumped out of the carriage with as much bounce as Isaiah had displayed earlier, and held out his hand to her.

*The root of the wind,* Emily thought . . . *the root of the wind . . .*

## 28

*S*he evening was so fine that Emily insisted they take a drive before darkness came. Otis instructed the driver to continue on past the Messassoit to Stearns' Park. Though Emily still wore black she had wrapped herself in her heliotrope shawl, and as the early evening was also wrapped in heliotrope, her eyes seemed lighted with the color. The window was down and the wind, though soft, stirred the unbound bits of her hair about her face, and as she pushed them back she laughed.

"I am so happy," she said.

He took her hand in his and smiled at her. "The week wasn't too difficult for you?"

"It was difficult and wonderful at the same time. And sad and happy and bliss, as well." She laughed, delighted as a young schoolgirl. "It has been ecstasy!"

He grew very serious. "I have reached a decision—" he began.

She could not control her laughter. "You look exactly like an owl. That's what father used to call you— the wise owl. I shall remember that, and in the evenings when you are not by my side, I shall go out into the night and talk to owls, with the idea that you might well be playing tricks on me!"

"Are you going to listen, Emily?"

"Oh—" Emily said, smiling, like a child realizing it was being reprimanded. "Darling Salem, please continue."

"I am retiring from the bench."

Emily was not quite prepared for this, and confusion paled her face and her smile flickered and then disappeared. "It isn't because of me?" she asked in a thin voice, drawing her shawl even closer about her as though suddenly feeling a chill.

He sensed immediately the fear she felt and patted her hand to reassure her and smiled quite openly and adoringly into her eyes. "No, of course not," he said. "It is something I have been considering for some time, but this week—this sad case—seemed to help me decide. I would like to return to private practice."

The tension eased in her and she gave a nervous but thankful little sigh. "I was surprised, that was all. You never mentioned you were considering such a move. Of course, if you prefer private practice, I think you should step down as soon as possible."

"I feel I will be more useful that way," he argued in his own behalf, "and able to make a more important contribution."

She smiled again, and seeing that he needed reassuring, brought forth all her latent maternal instincts. "Of course! You are right! But, darling Salem, all those troubled people relying on you!" She sighed heavily. "I only hope I can ease your burden in some small way."

He was immediately under her spell. "Just being near me, Emily, that is sufficient." The curtain was drawn back, so that occupants in other carriages could see in. He looked a little flustered, undecided, and then he raised her hand to his lips and kissed it.

The driver drew up before Stearns' Park. Young people dotted its lanes. Emily could not help thinking about Maud Hagarty and how changed her life was now —how impossible it would be for her to stroll in this park with girlish abandon. "Let's go on," she suggested, her change of mood obvious.

"Where?" he asked indulgently.

"Oh, the riverbank."

He gave the instructions to the driver and at the same time shut the window and drew the curtain. Then he took her in his arms and a great feeling of comfort encompassed them both. She leaned back against his chest and he stroked her hair.

"Henry has offered me a partnership," he said at last in the darkness of the cab. "That would mean living in Springfield. Would you like that?"

She thought about it for a moment. "Sweet hours have perished here—" she said softly. "Yes, I would like that very much."

"I thought we could be married in June."

"Not in Amherst?"

"Not if you prefer elsewhere."

"Here, I think."

"It would be too soon to find a proper house."

"Perhaps," she whispered shyly, "perhaps we would then have time for a honeymoon."

"Of course!" He hugged her to him.

The carriage had stopped, and he sat up straight and released her and drew back the curtain. Night had fallen. One could hear the river but not see it. He helped her out of the carriage. There was a moon and a complement of stars and the city was dazzling, but the river was concealed by the shadows of the railway cars and the height of the factory buildings.

"I am afraid this is the wrong stretch of riverbank," he said, and started to assist her back into the carriage.

However, she remained standing, looking straight ahead, and he turned his glance to what she saw.

Dozens of chimneys jutted into the night sky. It was the Smith and Wesson Arms plant. Behind and beyond the dark brick walls and the blackened chimneys, was Springfield—bright with streetlamps. They stood together, both thinking about the trial and the Kidder family and their hopes that were now like shadows in a tomb.

"I can't help thinking about Charles Kidder . . ." she began.

He clasped her hand in a sign of mutual understanding and they returned to the carriage.

"The Messassoit," the judge told the driver. He sat well back in the darkened interior and drew Emily to him. *"How do I love thee? Let me count the ways,"* he whispered. "Browning, I believe."

*"That love is all there is, is all we know of love,"* she whispered back. "Dickinson," and smiled, and then, settling her head on his shoulder, added, "Soon to be Mrs. Jumbo Lord."

And the carriage took them through the tender early-spring night and delivered them with the greatest discretion at their destination.

> *Morning is due to all—*
> *To some—the Night—*
> *To an imperial few—*
> *The Auroral light.*

# Return to Amherst

*Had I known that the first was the last*
*I should have kept it longer.*
*Had I known that the last was the first*
*I should have drunk it stronger.*
*Cup, it was your fault,*
*Lip was not the liar.*
*No, lip, it was yours,*
*Bliss was most to blame.*

*A*ustin had met them at the
station and driven them home. It was only a few minutes' ride, but in that time Emily sensed the breach between Austin and Sue. They spoke politely to each other,
kissed perfunctorily upon meeting, and smiled stiffly.
Could love grow tired and want to sleep, hungry and
need to graze? It seemed to do so with the love between
Austin and Sue, and it pained Emily to think of that love
that had been cherished for so long and had begun in
such joy, to fall away like dried clay and prove mortal
after all.

She and Sue had been in such high spirits on the
train trip to Amherst. It had taken them back to the time
when they had been young girls together and shared
secret confidences. Sue would be her ally in the difficult
days ahead, for she knew Vinnie and Austin would re-
sist. Now she fervently hoped her plan would not cause

the distance between Sue and Austin to widen so that there could no longer be a footpath between them.

Austin stopped at his house first. The carriage was immediately stormed by the three children, who all but lifted their mother out.

"I will be up to the house later," Sue assured Emily when she found both her breath and a moment of comparative quiet. Then she was whisked away by the children toward their front doors amid shouts of "Did you bring a surprise?"

"Me," she heard Sue reply.

"No! In the suitcase, in the suitcase!" little Gilbert insisted.

Then they were out of earshot. It was a fine open carriage that Austin had purchased only a week before her trip to Springfield, and Dapper, Austin's proud mare, drew it along regally. Yes, green had come to Amherst, too. It was everywhere you looked. Spring had officially arrived and brought a bit of madness with it. She had climbed into Austin's open rig and never considered the consequence. But then, who cared for consequence now? However, since they had arrived at noon, no one had been on the streets. The irony of frivolity!

Austin was silent for the few moments it took to go from his house to her father's house. It was unlike him, and Emily sensed something faraway and deeply troubled in his attitude. Her heartbeat quickened as the thought occurred to her that her own loved one might have been in a similar dilemma those many years ago when Elizabeth had joined him in Boston. She dismissed the thought quickly and concentrated on the babble of the birds, the wild assortment of smells, and the tingle of the rushing spring air.

Vinnie met them at the door. "Welcome home, Sister," she said curtly. Kissing Emily lightly on the cheek, she took her handbag and turned away as though intent on carrying it straightaway upstairs.

"I'll take care of that, Vinnie," Emily said slowly. "First I think Austin wants to return home."

Vinnie lowered the case to the floor. "How good of him," she replied with a touch of acid in her voice and then stood with a forced smile on her face. Apparently Vinnie had either heard about Austin's liaison or guessed something of the sort, and it rested sorely with her.

The door was still open and Austin edged his way back to it. "I will leave you to rest now, Emily," he said. Then he was gone.

The two sisters faced each other in the front hallway.

"The world seems to have gone mad," Vinnie said, but it was more of a cry and it seemed that she was on the very edge of breaking.

"Why, Vinnie, Vinnie dear." Emily went immediately to her sister's side.

"Don't touch me," Vinnie ordered. She began to cry, but turned away so that Emily would not see her face.

"Vinnie, is it Austin? Or you? Or Mother? Can it be me? What is it, Vinnie?" Emily asked gently.

Vinnie turned sharply and faced her. There was something marionettelike in the way she moved and spoke and in the exaggerated gestures, the strained voice, the tight curls about her face, the dress that looked like a theater costume.

*Oh, Lord,* Emily thought, *we have been living such a baroque life.*

"How curious you should ask," Vinnie was saying venomously. "How could you? How ever could you have gone off as you did? Sometimes I don't think I know you at all, Emily Dickinson! Leaving without consulting me! Leaving Mother! Forcing Sue to be absent from Austin at a most *crucial* time in their marriage! Going to Springfield and staying with— Oh! Dear, dear!" She wrung her hands, and as she did, a small scream emerged.

"Vinnie—" Emily attempted to take her hand, but Vinnie pulled it back and away and wiped it on her skirt.

"Such, such *commonness*. You met Otis Lord. I know it! I know it!" Vinnie collapsed on the bottom step in a heap of shaking muslin and with an eruption of uncontrolled tears.

Emily stood looking at her, shocked and silent. She had never quite thought of Vinnie as she did this moment—self-absorbed, selfishly remote from reality, knowing and caring little for the love and despair of others.

Finally Vinnie's sobs subsided, and Emily said, "This is not the right way or the way I intended to tell you this, Vinnie, but Otis Lord and I are to be married in June in Springfield, and we will make our home there." She had blurted it out because she felt she had to bring Vinnie to her senses and could think of no other way except truth.

Vinnie's face grew very pale and she clutched at her heart as though she might be suffering an attack, looking up at Emily with wide, disbelieving eyes. "It can't be," she whispered. Her face sagged tragically, her lips quivered. But then she braced herself, and though her breath was short, she gasped the words "What is to become of me?"

Emily dropped down on her knees beside her. "Perhaps you can come to Springfield too, dear. Or take a trip with Sue. She spoke of that possibility."

"And Mother?"

"I know, I know, dear. I am going to speak to Austin about that. I think we should look for a nurse-companion. I am sure it will be quite possible to find someone very trustworthy."

Vinnie rose slowly to her feet, and Emily after her. They were an arm's length apart. Lines of determination formed around Vinnie's mouth and a hardness came into her eyes. "It won't come to pass," she said. "The Lord will make a very great thunder."

For the first time since she had entered the house, a smile flickered on Emily's face. "He already has, Vinnie," she said. "He already has."

Otis returned home feeling younger than he had in years, thinking he could take on anything. Therefore, after the joyous welcomes had subsided and he had rested for an hour, he called the two Farley ladies to him in his library and proceeded in a direct fashion to tell them his plans for the immediate future.

It was the twilight hour, a time of day the judge never had liked, and he had lighted all the lamps, and the candles as well, so that the room was bathed in light. Attempting a casual air, he stood in front of the fireplace, and having insisted that the two ladies be seated, had *shared* his good news with them.

Neither lady was capable of an immediate reply. They exchanged desperate glances. Abbie rose slowly and spoke first. "If this will make you happy, Uncle, then of course you know you have my good wishes," she said in a stiff, awkward manner, her face the color of moonstone in the harshness of the room's light.

Her mother rose nervously and placed her tremulous fingers on her daughter's arm for support. "My good wishes, too," she said weakly, and then swayed forward. Otis steadied her. "Oh, dear," she gasped and then, unable to control herself any longer, began to cry bitterly.

Abbie and Otis eased her back into the chair, but she

could not stanch her sobs. She looked a trifle foolish, as some people do when they cry, and she was stammering incoherently between sobs something about her sister Elizabeth.

"What about Elizabeth, Mary?" he asked gently.

"She promised! She promised!" She sobbed hysterically and her face twisted in anguish.

Abbie placed her own quivering hand on her mother's shoulder. "Mother," she admonished in a voice not completely under control. Then she straightened, and remembering her position and her training, disciplined her actions. It was as though someone had turned on a switch and lighted her cloudy thoughts. Her face was still moon-white and her eyes charred with disappointment. Still, when she spoke again, her voice was cool and low and her hand no longer trembled. "You must forgive Mother," she apologized. "It simply was too great a shock, coming suddenly as it did."

Mary choked back her sobs and began to whimper. Otis was pacing back and forth across the room, hands thrust behind his back, his thoughts in turmoil, his heart filled with hurt and dismay.

"Damn it! It is my life!" he bellowed, and Mary, terrified now, more shaken than anguished, swallowed dryly and looked even paler with fright.

"It is not my place to interfere, of course," Abbie began, gaining small courage in the face of desperation.

Her uncle spun about and faced her. "I could not wait to share my happiness with you," he said harshly. "But I can see now my happiness does not mean a fig to you!"

"No! No!" Mary protested. "Please! No angry words. It is so vulgar—so—Oh, dear!"

"Mother," Abbie warned.

"Where shall we go? Where shall we go?" her mother sobbed.

Otis drew a sharp breath and continued, refusing to submit to the woman's hysteria. "You both may keep this house. It never was my home." He started for the door. He was breathing very heavily. "But while I am still in it, I do not want to speak to you upon this subject again." He paused at the door and glowered at them. "I shall dine alone. Have Cora serve me in this room when you have vacated it." Then he turned and was gone.

*E*mily sat down noiselessly on the chair beside her mother's bed. Her mother had dozed off, and so Emily closed the Bible and waited. She did not quite know what she waited for, but she felt impelled to remain. She had told her mother of her plans to marry, watched her face closely to see how she took the news. A smile had quivered on her lips for only a brief moment and then flickered out—a candle in the wind, seeming dead now, waxen.

There had been a curious character to that fleeting smile. Emily knew it wasn't meant for her, and as though touched with the ability to sense others' thoughts, she pondered on why her mother should find satisfaction toward her father in the news. For the smile had clearly said, *"There, Edward, you see!"* Sleep had come easy after that, for she had felt at peace.

It was the first time Emily had given any thought at all to the union that had brought her into the world. Had there been love between these two people she believed she had known so well? The kind of love that she shared with Otis? She was aware that few people loved at all, and she was saddened to think her mother might have been one of those.

*There, Edward, you see* . . .

Reproachfulness had surfaced in that smile, derisiveness. It was a smile that accused and yet at the same time was smug in its judgment.

Images flashed in Emily's mind. Her mother's taut, drawn mouth, her stony glance at her father when he brought her home from school. Her mother had not dared speak, but her disapproval of that act was suddenly, and after all these decades, very clear to Emily.

Another vision: a young professor from the College came to call, to say his farewell to her because he had lost his post and so was forced to leave Amherst. She had been desolate, for he had been one of the few young men she could communicate with. Her father had stood implacable, never leaving them alone, but her mother . . . she had brought them refreshments and there had been tears in her eyes.

It was with shocking clarity that Emily now realized that this woman whom she thought to be so cold, so indifferent all her life, had loved her with an intensity that had caused her to retreat to silence.

There were carriage sounds outside the window, and Emily rose to see who it might be. Austin was stepping down from the driver's seat. Oh, yes, today Austin was taking a train to Cambridgetown for a meeting. In her pocket was a letter she had written to Otis, and she hurried to the door to ask him to post it for her.

She turned for a fleeting moment at the door, and glanced at her mother. The smile had returned to her lips. Emily opened the door, but before she left the room she patted the letter in her pocket.

*There, Edward,* she said under her breath, *you see* . . .

Vinnie stood in the downstairs hall, her cloak on, her bonnet tied.

"I had thought I might ride into town with Austin," Vinnie said, her eyes wide, somehow alarmed as she watched her sister descend the stairway, a certain new lift to her step, clutching the Bible in one hand, a letter in the other.

"Perhaps you wouldn't mind posting this for me, then," Emily asked, and handed Vinnie the letter.

Vinnie took it silently from her. They had hardly exchanged a word during the entire weekend, since Emily's return. She looked at Vinnie now with pleading eyes, as though to say *Please share my happiness.* But Vinnie turned away and hurried to Austin's side.

"I brought the Springfield *Republican* for you," he said to Emily after a quick and cold glance to Vinnie.

"Well, thank you, Austin," Emily replied with some surprise. Generally Austin did not bring the newspaper until he had read it, and Emily noted that it was that day's edition and the day still early.

He held the paper in his outstretched hand. She took it with very little further thought and put it on the hall table. "How are Sue and the children?" she inquired.

"Fine. Sue will be up shortly." He remained standing, seeming uncertain, awkward.

Vinnie grabbed his arm and they left and Emily went into the kitchen. She could see them through the window, having what seemed like an exchange of harsh words. Finally, Austin climbed up on his carriage alone and Vinnie turned back to the house. Emily, sensing some impending crisis, hurried to the hallway just as Vinnie flung the door open, gasping for breath, her hand trembling as she removed her bonnet.

"Did you see anything in the paper that concerned us, Emily?" she asked.

"Why, no, Vinnie. I hardly have had time to read it."

Emily came further into the hallway. The folded newspaper sat where she had left it, but from this distance any newsprint that was visible was blurred. "What is it, Vinnie?" she managed, her heart already beating wildly.

"Mr. Lord . . ." Vinnie began.

Emily moved toward the table, but her legs felt leaden. She picked up the paper and clutched it to her as she waited for an explanation from Vinnie, unable to bring herself to read whatever it was for herself. Vinnie's silence said it all. Emily's sight suddenly failed her and her body grew cold. The doorbell rang and Sue ran in.

"Oh, Emily, Emily dear," she cried in a strange voice.

The two women stood clasped in each other's arms, Emily sobbing as Sue rocked her back and forth as she might have done one of her children.

"Don't cry," Vinnie said nervously. "I cannot stand to see you cry." Emily, controlling her sobs, moved away from Sue. Now there was pride in her bearing and strength in her eyes. She looked at Sue and Vinnie. She studied the hallway very carefully. She made a note of how the light came through the windows at this time of day. Then she went into the kitchen and went about her daily tasks.

But Emily knew that Otis would not survive.

*I stepped from Plank to Plank*
*A slow and cautious way*
*The Stars about my Head I felt*
*About my Feet the Sea.*

*I knew not but the next*
*Would be my final inch—*
*This gave me that precarious Gait*
*Some call Experience.*

## 31

Emily once again clothed herself in white. Weeks, months, finally a few years passed. She welcomed few people and withdrew more and more into her own world.

Mrs. Dickinson had died in 1882, and Lavinia and Emily lived in the house alone. There was a great tenderness between them now. Much of the time Emily remained in her room, looking out the west window, reading, penning letters and poems. The poems she still tied in small packets and hid in her bureau drawer.

In the spring, four years after Otis Lord's heart seizure, Emily fell ill. One evening Vinnie brought supper to Emily's bedside. Vinnie seemed frightened. Emily took her sister's warm hand and steadied its trembling in her own weak grasp.

"Vinnie," she whispered, "you lose something, but get something else in return, even if only a sense of loss. It was that way with me and it will be that way for you."

"You are not to talk such nonsense, Emily Dickinson!" Vinnie scolded.

A faint smile appeared on Emily's face. Then it flickered out and she tightened her grasp on Vinnie's hand, this time holding it with both her own. "Vinnie, in the top drawer of my bureau there are some packets —poems and letters. Destroy the letters, but keep the poems."

"I told you, Emily Dickinson—"

"There's no time for charades, Vinnie—promise me?"

"I promise," Vinnie managed.

"And, Vinnie dear, put a sprig of heliotrope in my hand so that I can take it to Judge Lord." Her eyes closed and her hand grew slack.

"Emily!" Vinnie screamed.

But Emily had lost consciousness, and she died at six that evening, at twilight. She was carried from her father's house wearing white and holding a sprig of heliotrope, and was buried by her father's side. The poem of Emily Brontë's that she so admired was read by Thomas Higginson at the close of the funeral service.

At home, Vinnie, alone, went to Emily's room, opened the bureau drawer, and found all those paper scraps with Emily's writing on them, tied together with bits of ribbon. She could not believe her eyes. There were almost a thousand poems.

It took her a long time to read the poems and to go through the letters as well. Vinnie did not know what to do, for many of the poems seemed to refer specifically to Otis Lord and to Emily's intense feeling for him. Emily had said *Destroy the letters, but not the poems.* But now her sister's instruction posed too great a responsibility, so Vinnie took all the papers to Austin.

Of the family, only Sue was not surprised at the contents of Emily's bureau drawer, but in the end it was Austin who made the final decision to lock away all the poems and letters that might be embarrassing, with instructions that they be withheld until all members of the immediate family were deceased. As for the less sensitive material, he would seek publication at once.

Austin had much to think about after Vinnie's departure. Emily was gone, but a curious essence remained. Tears filled Austin's eyes. Emily . . . *Emily*—she was revealed to him now for the first time since they had shared youth.

> *There is another sky,*
> *Ever serene and fair,*
> *And there is another sunshine*
> *Though it be darkness there;*
> *Never mind faded forests, Austin,*
> *Never mind silent fields—*
> *Here is a little forest,*
> *Whose leaf is ever green,*
> *Here is a brighter garden,*
> *Where not a frost has been;*
> *In its unfading flowers*
> *I hear the bright bee hum;*
> *Prithee, my brother,*
> *Into my garden come!*

# Afterword

This novel is based on a crucial relationship in the life of Emily Dickinson, one of America's three or four great poets. A great deal has been written about Miss Dickinson's "queerness." For many years of her life she was a recluse, and, in Amherst, Massachusetts, where she lived, as well as in the rest of New England, there was an enormous amount of speculation about her life. She was surrounded by rumor, and as it turns out, much of that rumor was manufactured by those closest to her in order to conceal what they considered to be the scandalous truth. Such stories as Miss Dickinson's unrequited love for Charles Wadsworth, a Philadelphia clergyman, grew out of just this sort of deliberate invention.

Perhaps the truth about Emily Dickinson's private life would never have seen the light had it not been for her brother Austin's own indiscretion. Married and the father of three children, Austin fell in love with a young married woman who lived in Amherst with her husband, who was employed at the College. Mabel Todd Loomis, the lady in question, was fascinated by the world of literature and eager to be a part of it. Emily's death provided her with that opportunity.

After Emily died, Lavinia Dickinson, Emily's sister, brought to her brother Austin the hundreds of poems and letters she had found in Emily's bureau drawer. The family decided to seek publication, but to protect Emily and her hidden life, they felt that only someone close to the family could be trusted with the editing. Austin gave this task to Mabel Todd Loomis and he also gave her Emily's letters to Judge Otis Lord of Salem, Massachusetts. These letters revealed the passion which Emily Dickinson and Otis Lord had shared.

Working with Thomas Higginson, editor of the *Atlantic Monthly* magazine, Mrs. Loomis altered punctuation and pronouns in the poems—often changing *he* to *she*. She also held back from publication all poems which might be "misinterpreted." Then she took the packet of the duplicates of Emily's own letters to Otis Lord, which Emily had kept, and placed them in a trunk. (Lavinia Dickinson had already destroyed Judge Lord's letters to Emily.)

And so, with no real evidence available, false legends about Emily Dickinson grew and were nurtured until Mabel Todd Loomis' death in 1932, forty-six years afer Emily had died. The packet of letters then came into the hands of Millicent Todd Bingham, Mabel's daughter. It was with great shock that Mrs. Bingham recognized what a treasure she had inherited. She decided to reveal the truth to the world, but it was not an easy task, and assembling the material occupied her for twenty-two years. Finally, in 1954, the letters were published in a book called *Emily Dickinson—A Revelation*, with Mrs. Bingham listed as author. Curiously, because so many books had already been published romanticizing the apparently loveless lady poet, the public was slow to believe the documented facts.

To write this novel, I have drawn upon Emily's

letters and upon those aspects of her personality and character revealed in her poems. Her work and, I hope, this book make clear the fact that not only was Emily Dickinson a great artist, she was also a complete and fulfilled woman. The book is not a biography, of course, but much of the contents has been drawn from authentic documents and much of the dialogue attributed to Emily is a paraphrase of her own words. I have used this material taking a novelist's liberty in weaving it into a story, but, for example, the Kidder trial was in fact presided over by Judge Lord at a time when he and Emily could finally confess their love and make plans to be married. The judge did suffer a heart seizure directly after that period.

I would like to thank Mrs. Gladys Porter of the Essex Institute in Salem; the staff in charge of Genealogy and Archives in the Springfield Library; the library staff of the Springfield Courthouse, for the Kidder trial manuscripts; the staff of the Stockbridge and Lenox libraries, who were enormously helpful in obtaining research material for me; Amherst College, and individuals like Mr. Gilbert Cohen and my daughter, Catherine Edwards, who helped me gather data.

And last, my most grateful appreciation to the Harvard University Press, which granted me the permission for the use of the poems and letters of Miss Dickinson that appear in this book; and to Houghton Mifflin and Little Brown for their kind cooperation in allowing the appearance of those poems, in which they hold joint copyright.

Anne Edwards
Stockbridge, Massachusetts
1973